D0662019

New Business Networking
How to Effectively Grow Your Business Network
Using Online and Offline Methods

DAVE DELANEY

800 East 96th Street,
Indianapolis, Indiana 46240 USA

New Business Networking

ISBN-13: 978-0-7897-5098-3
ISBN-10: 0-7897-5098-8

Library of Congress Control Number: 2013935188

Printed in the United States of America

First Printing: May 2013

Trademarks

Warning and Disclaimer

Bulk Sales

Que Publishing offers excellent discounts on this book when ordered in quantity for bulk purchases or special sales. For more information, please contact

U.S. Corporate and Government Sales
1-800-382-3419
corpsales@pearsontechgroup.com

For sales outside of the U.S., please contact

International Sales
international@pearsoned.com

Editor-in-Chief
Greg Wiegand

Senior Acquisitions Editor
Katherine Bull

Marketing Manager
Dan Powell

Development/
Technical Editor
Amber Avines

Managing Editor
Kristy Hart

Senior Project Editor
Lori Lyons

Copy Editor
Karen Davis

Senior Indexer
Cheryl Lenser

Proofreader
Dan Knott

Editorial Assistant
Cindy Teeters

Interior Designer
Anne Jones

Cover Designer
Alan Clements

Senior Compositor
Gloria Schurick

Que Biz-Tech
Editorial Board
Michael Brito
Jason Falls
Rebecca Lieb
Simon Salt
Peter Shankman

CONTENTS AT A GLANCE

Table of Contents

5   Building a Network, 140 Characters at a Time: Twitter   71

About the Author

Dave Delaney is a recognized leader, consultant, and speaker on digital marketing, social media strategy, and business networking.

Delaney began his career in marketing, promotions, and publicity in Toronto, Ontario, Canada working in performing arts publicity and marketing, newspaper promotions, and broadcast television marketing. In Nashville, Tennessee, his career switched to technology-focused companies where he managed digital marketing efforts focusing on social media strategy and execution.

He hosted one of the first parenting podcasts from 2005–2008, and he has been blogging for nearly a decade.

Dave co-founded two annual unconferences, PodCamp Nashville and BarCamp Nashville. He has also launched two monthly networking events, Nashcocktail and Geek Breakfast. The latter now has chapters across the United States, Canada, South Africa, and Australia.

In July 2012, Delaney was selected by *Billboard Magazine* as a digital marketing expert to follow. Dave Delaney has appeared in technology stories in *USA Today*, *Billboard Magazine*, *Globe & Mail*, *Nashville Business Journal*, *The Tennessean*, and *Mashable*.

Delaney frequently speaks at private events, functions, and public conferences. Engagements include South by Southwest Interactive, Social Media Club Nashville, American Marketing Association Nashville, Interlogix Partners Conference, Killer Tribes, Explore, PodCamp Toronto, BarCamp Nashville, and PodCamp Nashville.

Dedication

It took less than a millisecond for me to know who this book is dedicated to: Heather. My wife and best friend. Your belief, encouragement, patience, love, and support knows no bounds. Sam and Ella, this book is also for you. I hope it helps guide you through your careers, but for now go back to playing and being silly. You will have plenty of time to be grown-ups later. I love you three with all of my heart.

Acknowledgments

Thank you to Katherine Bull, Amber Avines, Lori Lyons, and Karen Gill for their collective wisdom and guidance, and to the entire staff at Que and Pearson for believing in me.

When I was in high school and void of direction, George and Maureen Delaney, Bob Elhart, Timothy Snelgrove, and Steve Berry all met with me to brainstorm, review my resume, and help guide me in the right direction. I got sidetracked a few

times along the road but without their early guidance, I may never have found my way.

I have had many informational meetings throughout my career, and each led to a new idea, introduction, or opportunity. Thank you to: Carrie, John, Young In, Loren, Jamie, Karen, Hannah, Clint, Marcus, Mark, Kate, Nicholas. To Sharon, Scoot, Skinny, Sims, who pushed me when I needed pushing back in Hogtown.

To fellow authors and friends who inspire me every day: John, C.C., Julien, Mitch, Chris, Jason, Amber, Seth, Chris. To my countless friends, fans, and followers online and offline. You keep me going.

To the city of Nashville, Tennessee, who welcomed me with open arms. To attendees of Geek Breakfast and Nashcocktail, and friends who have carried on PodCamp Nashville and BarCamp Nashville. I am so lucky to call Nashville my home. What you hear about southern hospitality is alive and well in Music City.

To my Mum, Dad, and Mike. For your love and support. To my incredible wife and best friend, Heather. Without your love and patience, this book would not be...I would not be. To Sam and Ella, you two are the light of my life.

We Want to Hear from You!

As the reader of this book, *you* are our most important critic and commentator. We value your opinion and want to know what we're doing right, what we could do better, what areas you'd like to see us publish in, and any other words of wisdom you're willing to pass our way.

We welcome your comments. You can email or write to let us know what you did or didn't like about this book—as well as what we can do to make our books better.

Please note that we cannot help you with technical problems related to the topic of this book.

When you write, please be sure to include this book's title and author as well as your name and email address. We will carefully review your comments and share them with the author and editors who worked on the book.

Email: feedback@quepublishing.com

Mail: Que Publishing
            ATTN: Reader Feedback
            800 East 96th Street
            Indianapolis, IN 46240 USA

Reader Services

Visit our website and register this book at quepublishing.com/register for convenient access to any updates, downloads, or errata that might be available for this book.

1

Do Your Homework

Oh, no! What did I do? I helped my wife, Heather, load up all our belongings and our 3-month-old daughter and 14-month-old son to move down to Tennessee from Toronto. I don't know anyone down there. I don't have a job lined up, and I have no one to help me land on my feet. Okay, Delaney. It's time to get serious.

We stored our belongings and moved in with my in-laws in Jackson, Tennessee. It was up to me to network intensively so that we could eventually make the move from my in-law's home in Jackson to our own home in Nashville.

I spent the bulk of my days in Jackson at a local coffee shop with free Wi-Fi. As many early entrepreneurs will agree, coffee shops with free Wi-Fi are essential to growing a business. Of course, the caffeine helps, too. Without a great coffee shop to go to, it's easy to get distracted by family or a roommate at home.

I researched job openings in all the regular places online: Monster.com, CareerBuilder.com, HotJobs.com, and Craigslist.com. These sites are good for finding some positions, but they are not optimal for everyone. I was getting nowhere, growing frustrated, and contemplating my career thus far.

In Toronto, I had built my career in the marketing industry. When we left Toronto, I was working in marketing and promotions for CanWest Media Works—specifically, Global Television. I'll tell you more about how I ended up at one of Canada's largest television networks in Chapter 2, "It Starts with a Coffee."

I knew I wanted to work in marketing for a media company in Nashville, but I could not find open positions listed on the job sites for these types of companies. I knew I would have to find another way. I realized that to find a job in Nashville, I would have to learn everything I could about the appropriate companies and people there. As you read my story, think about where you want to be. Take a moment to jot down some ideas.

GEEKING OUT SINCE 1984

Back in 1984, I ran a bulletin board system on my Commodore 64. I was a kid getting a true taste of the future of online communication. I was always excited to connect with people online. That screeching sound of a dial-up modem still delights me to this day.

In 1999, I started a social dating site in Galway, Ireland, called Spotted Galway. It was similar to the "Sightings" sections of many alternative weekly papers. The concept was simple: You saw someone you fancied at a pub, school, or club, and you left a message trying to connect with them. It was fascinating to watch users log in and use the service. I had thousands of regular users. I ended up selling the service to a British company when we moved back to Toronto.

From 2005 until 2008, Heather and I started one of the first parenting podcasts called "Two Boobs and a Baby." The popular Internet radio show was a big success. Each week, we would share our trials and tribulations from becoming first-time parents and soon second-time. We had a fantastic group of dedicated listeners who frequently posted comments on our blog and in our parenting forums. Our podcast chronicled our early years as parents, and even our move from Toronto to Tennessee in 2007.

I have always been interested in building community and connecting online. The Internet has given us the freedom to create amazing content and share and shape it openly. We live in a time when we can easily research the companies and people we want to connect with. Branding ourselves online is a perfect way to get the ball rolling.

It occurred to me that I had been blogging about marketing and culture since 2004. I realized that a blog was going to be a key way for me to do my homework about who and what was waiting for me in Nashville. I often tell students that they should start a blog before they graduate, because they are being taught and creating valuable information that is worth sharing. By starting a blog, you establish yourself.

When I first moved to Tennessee in January 2007, and started job hunting, I launched a blog called "New Media Nashville." As I mentioned, the purpose was to educate myself about Nashville's new media space. This included traditional media like print, radio, and television, but it also included new media like blogs, social networks, and podcasts. I needed to do extensive research to find the people and companies I wanted to connect with in my job hunt. I shared my findings on my blog to not only record my research, but to also establish myself in the community.

I spent countless hours researching local blogs, newsgroups, forums, newspapers, radio, and television stations. Google was my really good friend as I discovered stories related to Nashville's new media community.

Research was key to writing about Nashville's new media market on New Media Nashville. Keeping in mind that I didn't know a soul, I realized it would be best to learn about the companies I wanted to work for first. Researching the people I needed to connect with would be next, followed by local events I should attend.

I began with a simple spreadsheet to help me keep track of my networking. My downloadable spreadsheet can be found at http://bit.ly/NBNsimpledb. Yours doesn't have to be complicated. Mine wasn't. I suggest the following sections:

> First Name
> Last Name
> Email
> Company Name
> Company Address
> Company URL
> Twitter
> Facebook
> LinkedIn
> How Can I Help Them?
> How Can They Help Me?
> Meeting Status
> Outcome
> Follow-Up

Not only did I learn a lot about Nashville, but I began to get my name out to people in the community before I had even moved there. By blogging about Nashville, I was learning about the companies and people I wanted to meet. Blogging isn't for everyone, but having your space on the Web is. In Chapter 3, "Your Home on the Web Needs More Than a Welcome Mat," I'll write more about how to carve your space on the Web.

It was from writing my blog and having my place on the Web for potential employers to check me out that I found a full-time job (more about this in Chapter 2). However, the job didn't come until after I had spent plenty of time in face-to-face networking. Meeting people and growing your network is key to finding work, new clients, investors, and anyone else who will help you gain control over your career. An important bonus to actively growing your network is the friendships that occur. Without doing the work of finding interesting people, your paths may never cross otherwise.

Job Tips

Whether you are looking for a new job, graduating from college, finding investors for your start-up, or seeking clients for your business, you must know who is out there, or you are a ship without a sail. Begin by researching the companies that you want to work for or do business with.

 Tip

Don't settle on every company with an opening. By researching the companies, you can choose the ones that have the best cultures, benefits, people, products, and services that fit your style. You will spend at least 40 hours a week with the company you end up working with, so do your homework.

There are a number of resources that you can tap into to discover the companies around you:

- Your local area Chamber of Commerce is a good starting point. An array of different businesses all support chambers, many of which are publicly available on the chamber's site.
- Trade associations list businesses that are specific to an industry. The United States alone has more than 7,600 trade associations.[1] Wikipedia lists many of them at http://en.wikipedia.org/wiki/List_of_industry_trade_groups_in_the_United States.

- Check out small business associations. The U.S. Small Business Administration (www.sba.gov/) is a good resource. Also see the National Federation of Independent Business at www.nfib.com/.

- Look at who sponsors local events you are interested in. Once you find ones you want to explore, take note of who the sponsors are. Sponsors sponsor for a reason. They want to hear from you.

- Hoovers.com is a massive database of company and industry information. Portions are behind a paywall, but the free search is worth using to learn more about the companies you are interested in.

- Search for articles about the companies and your industry in your local paper and online.

- Read trade publications.

- Ask your friends and family for their recommendations.

- Google the industry you want to work in and the city you live in. For example: "advertising agency + Nashville."

- Visit your library, and ask a librarian for help with your quest to compile a list of advertising agencies in Nashville.

- Search for related groups and businesses on LinkedIn. You can find groups under the navigation bar. From there, choose Groups You May Like, or do a deeper search using Groups Directory. I will explain this further in Chapter 4, "Grow Your Network Before You Need It: LinkedIn."

- Attend local events related to your industry. I will elaborate on how to find these events in a moment.

Take note of the companies you want to work for or do business with, and add them to your spreadsheet. Your next step is to determine who it is you need to meet with at each company. If you want to work for the company, you need to meet the human resources manager or a senior-level person. If you want to do business with the company, you should try to learn who manages the department or company so you can speak to the decision maker.

Research People

Upon creating your dream list of companies in your spreadsheet, you will want to research who it is you should be meeting. For example, if you are seeking a marketing position, it's essential to find out who the chief marketing officer or marketing manager is.

If the company is publicly traded, it should be relatively easy to locate the name of the person you want to meet on the company website. If the company is private, you need to be more creative to track down the name. LinkedIn is a valuable resource for researching who does what in each company. Search for the company on LinkedIn, and select Employees. Then flip through the results until you find the appropriate person to contact. If you are already actively using LinkedIn, you may discover that you are connected to the person you want to meet. I'll write much more on LinkedIn in Chapter 4.

If you're a student, you probably have access to search engines like Lexis Nexus and Hoovers, which provide additional information that you likely won't find from a typical Google search. Hoovers often includes a list of senior managers for firms, annual earnings, and the company address. You are paying plenty for your education, so use the free tools and resources that come along with the package. Ask your campus librarian or research assistant for help. Non-students can also use Lexis Nexus' and Hoovers' basic search functions.

Search Google and the company website for press releases. These releases often include quotes from senior employees. Take note of how the publicist's email appears. You can usually find this format, so guessing the person's email is relatively easy.

Use the aforementioned spreadsheet, and be sure to include email addresses when possible. Most company email addresses are made up of a person's first name initial and last name @ the company name DOT com. For example, mine would be ddelaney@abusiness.com. Alternatively, the email address may be davedelaney@abusiness.com. If the company is small, it may simply be dave@abusiness.com.

You can find the people at the companies you need to connect with in several ways:

- Search the company name in Followerwonk (Followerwonk.com). This locates the name in any Twitter bio.
- Use LinkedIn to see who the current employees are at a company. From the careers page, choose to View All Employees.
- Check company press releases.
- Visit company websites, and look for the employee list or contact page.
- Read the company blog, and see who writes the content.
- Use the phone. Call the company, and ask who the marketing manager or head of human resources is.

The following sections describe other ideas that can help with your search.

Rapportive

One of the best free tools currently available is Rapportive. Rapportive is a social plug-in that you can add to your Gmail account. Once it is installed, a preview of the person you are emailing magically appears on the right side of your screen.

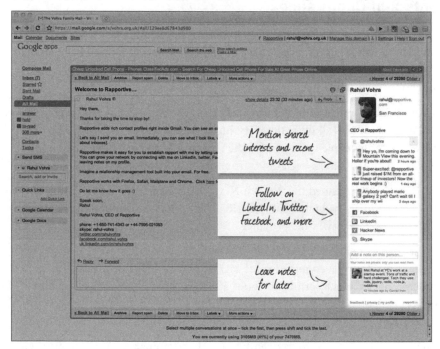

Figure 1.1   *Preview a person on Rapportive.com.[2]*

The Rapportive preview pulls information available from the person's email address. This usually includes the person's LinkedIn photo and account, Twitter tweets, and Facebook profile. It is a fantastic way to know who you are writing or replying to before clicking Send.

Rapportive is especially helpful when you are guessing a person's email address. It is also nice for getting to know someone a little more before you write the message. In fact, using it with LinkedIn may reveal that you are already connected through a mutual contact, and you can request an introduction instead of cold-emailing your contact.

By clicking in the Rapportive window's LinkedIn area, you can arrive directly on the person's LinkedIn account. You will see right away if you have any contacts who may know him. This is a perfect opportunity for you to learn a little more about this person and request an introduction from your contact.

At this point in the homework phase, you should have a good list of people and companies you want to connect with. One good way to meet these people casually is at conferences and events they plan to attend.

Events and Conferences

There is a popular web acronym called IRL, or in real life. This is an important term that I will mention repeatedly throughout this book. What I have learned through my many years connecting online is that online relationships become much more solidified once you have met a person IRL.

If you spend as much time as I do online, you are probably already seeking more IRL interactions. I call them the 3 Hs: high-fives, handshakes, and hugs. The feeling of meeting people in person for the first time is an incredible one, especially when you already know each other from online correspondences.

Back in 2007, I attended the Podcast New Media Expo in Ontario, California. This is where I add a small joke that Ontario, California, is nowhere near as lovely as Ontario, Canada, my home province.

My wife, Heather, and I had launched our successful parenting podcast "Two Boobs and a Baby" a couple of years earlier. Not only did we produce a weekly podcast, but I was subscribed to about 50 other shows. I am still a huge fan of the audio-on-demand format of podcasts. I listen to them more than music or the radio when I am traveling.

One program I listened to frequently was C.C. Chapman's, "Managing the Gray." Each episode of C.C.'s podcast included tips and tools to improve online marketing efforts. It was a great show that I looked forward to each week or two.

Not only did C.C. share valuable information in each episode, but he did it in a positive, inspiring way. His energy and passion for what would later be commonly known as "social media" was contagious.

C.C. and I had communicated through comments on his blog and social networking sites like Twitter, so we did know each other a bit but not very much. When I learned that he would be speaking at Podcast New Media Expo (PNME), I knew that we had to meet in person.

I remember specifically introducing myself to C.C. during one of the conference parties. He instantly produced a massive smile and threw out his arms to give me a hug. What an amazing way to meet a person who you admire and who you had only interacted with online.

The next morning, I attended his "Hey Homefries" breakfast, where I met an energetic group of podcasters. Not only did I get to hang out for breakfast with C.C.,

but I got to meet more incredible podcasting people like Charles Cadenhead, Paige Heninger, Molly Lynn, Ed Roberts, and Matthew Ebel. I also got to catch up with a fellow Canadian podcasting friend, Julien Smith, and met a popular blogger named Chris Brogan. Chris and Julien would later write a New York Times bestselling book, *Trust Agents*. They remain good friends today who have gone on to become leaders in social media marketing.

Figure 1.2   *C.C. Chapman's "Hey Homefries" breakfast at PNME 2007. From left, Matthew Ebel, C.C. Chapman, Julien Smith.*[3]

Today I consider C.C. a dear friend. When I asked him about his inspiration for his breakfast event, he explained, "That was so much fun. Of course, I didn't think of it as a networking event. I had a popular podcast and wanted to meet some of my listeners, so I invited everyone to breakfast. Sitting down over a meal is one of the best ways to get to know people, and I'm a huge fan of breakfast. So it was a fit."

By following C.C. on Twitter @cc_chapman, I knew he was going to the party. Are you following the people you want to meet on Twitter? Author Mitch Joel coined the term "permission-based stalking" when describing Twitter. I have always found it to be an appropriate and humorous definition. Had I not been following C.C., I would not have known where he would be that evening, and we would not have met in person. This meeting led to the breakfast that in turn introduced me to many other amazing people.

In Chapter 9, "If You Build It, They Will Come: Organizing Events," I'll talk more about how to organize your own events like C.C. did for his "Hey Homefries" breakfast. For now, let's talk about how to research the events that you should attend to connect and grow your network.

Finding Events

Not only is networking alone in your office ineffective, it is also kind of sad. You won't get far growing your network by sitting by yourself in your house. You need to get off your chair and into the world where other people are.

Some great sources of events are LinkedIn, Meetup, Facebook, Eventbrite, your local chamber of commerce, and newspapers. Let's explore some options and then talk more about conferences in general.

LinkedIn Events

One valuable feature of LinkedIn that many people miss is the Events section. Once logged in, you can navigate to the Events listing to find a variety of conferences that you may be interested in attending. After all, part of the value of any conference is the networking that takes place outside the auditorium, in the halls, cafes, and restaurants.

LinkedIn Events provides a list of seminars and conferences that are appropriate for you based on your professional network and LinkedIn profile. The algorithm actually selects events it thinks you will enjoy based on your job title and other key words used in your profile. I am always impressed with the quality of the results. If you don't see what you like, you can take it a step further by using the Events search engine.

A key feature of LinkedIn Events is that it reveals who in your network is attending the event. You can also see a list of other people who plan to attend. Decide who you want to meet during the event. Remember that you should always consider how you can help them first. Nobody likes a pushy sales guy, so never approach networking this way.

LinkedIn Professional is LinkedIn's paid service. You can see everyone who has been viewing your profile, which is a nice way to see who has found you. You can also see analytics to give you more information about how you appear in LinkedIn's search results. Paid users can use the InMail service to contact the people they want to meet. If you use LinkedIn's free service, you can also see a partial list of who has been viewing your profile and send five free InMails.

Beyond this, take advantage of Google. Simply search for the person and the name of their company. You will likely find a Twitter or Facebook profile associated

with the person. I will talk more about connecting on other social networking sites shortly. Add the contacts you want to meet to your spreadsheet. You will be using this to keep track, so don't forget to put it to good use.

It is expensive to travel to different cities to attend large conferences. Sometimes the best people to network with can be walking distance away. Local events can be a more cost-effective way to meet people closer to home.

Meetup

Meetup.com is a popular social networking site that was established in 2002 as a portal for finding and promoting local events.

Today there are 9.5 million members worldwide, with 92,000 monthly local groups based on 90,000 topics. Meetup can be found in 45,000 cities, with 280,000 organized meetups. Not bad, eh? The topics of the meetups range vastly, from book clubs and design groups to hiking and technology groups.

In early 2007, before officially moving to Nashville, I attended a meetup group about podcasting in Nashville. It was nice to connect with other locals who had a similar interest. Networking works well when you already have something in common. Like LinkedIn Events, Meetup usually shows the list of other attendees, so you can connect before the event.

The meetups do not always have to be specific to business networking for professional opportunities to present themselves. A key point to networking is to connect with a community of like-minded individuals. In Nashville, for example, Kelly Stewart started a meetup group for people interested in hiking in 2006. Today the group has over 5,000[4] members and is extremely active. Regardless of the group topic, relationships are built, and oftentimes business opportunities arise.

Actively networking can be exhausting, so it is important to choose wisely when deciding which events to attend. I have found that actual attendees versus registered attendees for free events is usually around 50%. If an event listed on Meetup has 40 people registered, I would expect 20 to actually show up. Paid events tend to have a higher conversion, because you lose your money if you buy a ticket and don't attend.

When you look through attendees of a Meetup event, they may include their social profiles. Check them out on Facebook, Twitter, and Flickr to learn a little about them. How can you help them? How can they help you? Add them to your list, and contact them before the event.

Let's say you see someone who is attending with a Twitter account. Review his latest tweets and Twitter bio. If you see something interesting, reply and follow him. You may want to add that you noticed he is attending the event and that you look forward to meeting him.

Facebook Events

There is no shortage of events listed on Facebook. Assuming you have a fair amount of friends, you should be able to see the upcoming events they are planning to attend. This may be a good reason to reach out to friends you haven't seen in a while. Find out where they will be by visiting www.facebook.com/events/list.

Use Facebook to ask your friends about the events you should be attending. What events are they planning to attend and why? Sometimes all it takes is asking the question.

Eventbrite

Eventbrite is best known as an online ticketing solution for event organizers. Not only is it excellent for this purpose, it is also a great resource of local events. Simply visit the Find Events section of the site and enter your city. Eventbrite then searches all public events coming up in your town. If you are searching for something to do tonight, Eventbrite also has a handy mobile app that can help you find events. Just go to www.eventbrite.com/eventbriteapp/.

Eventbrite uses Facebook Connect. By choosing to connect to Facebook, you will see your friends who are attending the events. This is a good opportunity to ask them more about why they are going or what they hope to get from the event.

Don't let an event frighten you if you don't know anyone attending. The purpose of networking is to connect with your contacts, but it is also to grow your network. You won't meet anyone new if you just stick with the people you know.

Chamber of Commerce and Other Sources

You will also find an array of local events listed in your local newspaper, alt. weeklies, Eventful.com, and chamber of commerce sites. Do some digging, and you are sure to find some great local events to attend.

Finding Conferences

Conferences are wonderful ways to connect with lots of people at one time. Ask your friends and colleagues which conferences they attend and why. Think about the areas you are most interested in to help you develop your career or business.

I have always enjoyed my time at South by Southwest (SXSW) Interactive, which has become the social media maven festival of the year. SXSW is an exception to many other conferences because of its sheer size. Each year approximately 25,000 people gather in Austin, Texas, in March to celebrate everything related to the Internet, from tech start-up entrepreneurs to video game enthusiasts.

Find the conference that is most appropriate for you, and do some research. If the event tickets are for sale on Eventbrite, you may be able to see who else will

be there. Many events have a Twitter hashtag associated with them. This is a great way to track the conversation before, during, and after the event.

USE TWITTER SEARCH TO CONNECT BEFORE, DURING, AND AFTER A CONFERENCE

Twitter hashtags are specific words used to track conversations on Twitter. By using Twitter's search function, you can search for hashtags specific to a conference. In the South by Southwest case, search for #SXSW or #SXSWi so you can meet and follow people discussing the conference. Don't forget to include the hashtag yourself when you are tweeting about an upcoming conference so other people can find you.

My experience is mainly with technology and marketing conferences, but not every type of conference attendee will use hashtags. However, they still may converse online about the conference. You can also set up and save a Twitter search for the conference name. I talk more about Twitter in Chapter 5.

Connecting with Others

Take note of the sponsors of events and conferences. They are sponsoring because they want their brand out there. They want to develop new business and possibly hire new staff. Why not contact the sponsors directly to find out more about their business? If you are interested, the sponsors will be more than willing to schedule a meeting during the conference. You may not get a job or a new client from the meeting, but you will be meeting someone new who works in an industry you are interested in. This is key to growing your network. Don't go looking for a job. Go because you genuinely want to learn more.

Connect with event organizers. They will be very busy as the event grows close. If you can introduce yourself early enough, you can learn more about how and why the event was created. The event organizer knows many people in the industry, so he would be a perfect person to connect with. Offer to help him promote the conference across your social channels, and ask him how you can help make it amazing.

Not all events and conferences are created equal. Consider this when deciding where to spend your time and money. If a local event has an open registration list and you only see a few people attending, it may not be worth your time. Also, if the event is for a topic that you are not really interested in, it may be worth reconsidering. Use your time wisely.

Try to connect with as many people as possible before the conference or event. By introducing yourself and establishing a relationship online, the meetings that you

schedule will be that much more productive and fun. Networking is a two-way street, so think about how you can help others.

Going with the Flow

Go with the flow at conferences. While I encourage you to do your best to pre-schedule meetings during conferences, I also recommend going with the flow. Some of my best memories from conferences were made during spur-of-the-moment gatherings.

One favorite story was during Gnomedex in Seattle in 2008. I was walking out of the conference center with a couple of friends when a graffitied school bus pulled up. The hosts invited us to hop in the Magic Bus so we could take a ride to a local art gallery.

The bus was filled with some of my favorite technology geeks in the world, like Dave Olsen, Chris Suspect, Amber Case, Kris Krug, Jacob Stewart, Alex Williams, Nathan Taylor, Pete Grillo, Scott Maentz, and Marcus Whitney.

The bus ride was a hilarious adventure through the side streets of Seattle. Most of us had no idea where we were going. We were too busy laughing at the absurdity of it all. Some of the people who were on the bus are still friends today. And it was all from going with the flow on a magic bus.

Another similar experience was during SXSW in 2007. I ran into Scott Monty, who would later become the social media manager for Ford Motor Company. Scott and I had been friends online for a while, but we had never met in person. We had just received our swag bags and badges and were looking for something to do. We both checked our phones and saw a tweet from the incredibly gifted cartoonist and author, Hugh MacLeod, also known as @gapingvoid on Twitter. Hugh suggested people join him for a pint on the patio of a bar across the street from the convention center.

Scott and I agreed that it was a fine idea indeed. We ventured across the street and joined a small group of Hugh's friends for a cold one. We then decided to see how many people we could attract to the bar from all of us tweeting our impromptu tweet-up. Within 30 minutes, we had about 50 people on the patio conversing excitedly about what SXSW had in store. Who knew that some of the people I met that day back in 2007 on the patio would still be friends?

Social Marketing

Social networking is all about building relationships with real people—not just brands, but the people behind the brands. The best businesses in social marketing understand this. They empower their employees to represent their brands across social channels.

That is the thing about networking. We are actively trying to connect with like-minded people. Sure, we are looking to grow our businesses and careers, but the importance of human relationships goes deeper than this. By attending events and meeting new friends or online friends in person, we are growing our professional networks, but we are also making our lives richer.

Endnotes

1. http://en.wikipedia.org/wiki/Trade_association

2. http://rapportive.com/about

3. Photo by Dave Delaney

4. http://celiasankar.com/blog/2011/11/16/meetup-ceo-talks-about-doing-what-you-love/

2

It Starts with a Coffee

In Chapter 1, "Do Your Homework," I wrote about how to research companies, people, and events to grow your network.

You have your spreadsheet with the names of the people you want to meet. Now is the time to consider how you will meet them. I used coffee, and you can, too.

I was working for a small performing arts publicity company. I was hired to help build a new sister company dedicated to selling group tickets to many of Toronto's small- to medium-sized theater companies. I was enjoying the job and the great people I worked with, but we hit a few too many roadblocks.

Unfortunately, it was decided that it was a bad time for group sales due to a number of matters out of the company's control. The company decided to cease operations, which meant I was about to be out of a job.

There are few things worse than being laid off, but it happens far more frequently than you think. If it has recently happened to you, I have some advice that worked for me. I hope it works for you, too.

Cold-Calling

While I was working for the publicity company, I was also studying business marketing in night classes and on weekends at one of Toronto's universities. One of my classes discussed the power of business networking and applying to work in memorable ways.

I knew that my time left at the company was short, so I had to find a way to start knocking on doors and meeting people. I researched the companies I wanted to work for. Most were in entertainment.

One such company was Alliance Atlantis, which was responsible for bringing amazing programs to Canadian television airwaves, like *The Sopranos*. By reading marketing trade magazines and digging into press releases on the company website, I found out who the marketing manager was.

I decided that cold-calling was going to be the best way to reach the marketing manager. I knew that if I could meet with him, I could learn more about the industry. That's a key point here in how we should be reaching out to people we don't know. Decide *why* you want to meet someone in the first place. Sure, we want to grow our networks, but we don't want to waste people's time either.

I have always found that asking to learn about the industry is a great request. Yes, I was certainly looking for a job. However, if you call someone and tell him you are looking for a job, he will redirect you to the human resources department or request that you send your resume. Put yourself in his shoes.

Because I was a part-time student, I decided that approaching networking as such made the most sense. I had determined that my *honest* story was that I was a student requesting to speak with the marketing manager about the television industry.

I can't stress enough that you need to approach networking honestly. What is your true story?

I learned quickly that persistence is key when trying to meet a senior person at a large company. Don't give up the first time you don't get a callback. Call again after a week if you haven't heard back. Always be polite if you are speaking with a personal assistant or receptionist. It is that person's job to be the gatekeeper and to block annoying unsolicited sales calls and the like.

Keep track of when you last called on your New Business Networking Simple Database (http://bit.ly/NBNsimpledb). If you have the person's email address, you

should look at his social profiles on Twitter, Facebook, Google Plus, and LinkedIn. Don't connect with him yet, but note his latest status updates. Perhaps he is going through some personal problems or is switching jobs.

One of two things is going to happen from cold-calling people:

1. They will never return your calls.

2. They will return your calls.

Let's look at both situations.

1. If they never return your calls, you can conclude that they are too busy to speak with you. Scratch those names off your list. Perhaps there is someone else you could connect with at the company. A chief marketing officer (CMO), vice president (VP), or president may be more welcoming. Don't be frightened by a fancy title. Everybody starts somewhere.

2. They returned your call! Awesome. This is exactly what you want and is what will happen most of the time. It's coffee time.

Remember that you are not meeting with the person for a job. Should a job offer come from the meeting, wonderful, but don't go expecting a job. Instead, be open to this new encounter. What you learn may open doors, but you may also learn ways that you can be of assistance. Always remember that networking is a two-way street. You need to offer to help others before assistance may return to you.

Go for these three reasons:

1. **To speak to the person about the industry.** What is the market like? How has the industry evolved in the past several years? What are some current trends? What is in store for the future?

2. **For an introductory, informational interview.** How did the person get into the industry? Where did she grow up? Where did she go to school, and what did she study? How long has she been working at company X? What are some milestones she has witnessed in her tenure?

3. **To ask about her company.** What are her favorite things about working for company X? How does it compare with her competition? How long has the company been around? Has it always been focused on this industry, or did it change its direction along the way? If so, why?

Do not show up to this informational interview unprepared. Know as much as you can about the person you are meeting by researching as outlined in Chapter 1. Don't be creepy with this information, but be aware of it. A look at a previous

position on LinkedIn may be worth bringing up if it seems fitting. For example, perhaps your contact previously worked with a company you are familiar with. You can ask what that experience was like.

Do your homework about the person's company and what she does there. What projects is she responsible for? What has the company recently done? Do a search on Google News to get some ideas, or look at the company's Facebook and LinkedIn pages.

The Coffee

When you get the person on the phone and ask for a brief meeting, be sure to include that you will bring a coffee.

"Thank you for speaking with me, Mr. Smith. I would appreciate a 15-minute meeting with you please. I am a marketing student here in Toronto, and I am really interested in learning more about the television and entertainment industries. I promise to bring you a coffee for your time."

"Thank you for your time, Mrs. Jones. I am a marketing professional who is new to town. May I take 15 minutes of your time to meet please? I would love to learn more about the city's marketing community and what you do at company X. I promise to bring you a coffee and take just 15 minutes of your time."

If the person pushes back and says he doesn't have the time, you can switch your request to 10 minutes. Be politely persistent. This is probably your only chance. I expect you will have a meeting scheduled by the end of your call. Assuming all goes well, be sure to email your contact after your call to thank him for his time. Remind him of the date and time he agreed to meet you in the email.

When it is meeting day, whatever you do, *don't forget the coffee!*

I once heard about a smart car dealership that was far out-selling its competition. If you have ever shopped for a new or used car, you are aware that several dealerships appear on the same street. It is a competitive business, so doing something special is key to being top of mind for potential customers.

The car dealership I mention used ice cream to win the hearts, souls, and cash from its customers. The idea is so simple you will slap your head.

Picture a hot Saturday in the summer. It is the busiest day of the week for dealers. Summer is also a perfect time to shop for a car. After showing potential customers their vehicles, most dealers would exchange handshakes, plug some sort of special financing offer, and hand you a business card. The dealership I am referring to did this, but it also handed you a large tub of ice cream. Who doesn't love ice cream?

Now picture yourself in the car shopper's shoes. It is summer, it is hot, and you are exiting a car lot with a tub of ice cream. Where is the first place you are heading? Home, directly to your freezer to save your melting dessert. Once home, you are less likely to pack the family in the old car and head back out to dealerships.

When you think back about the cars you saw during the day, the first thing you think about will be the last place you went. You will also remember the dealer who gave you the ice cream. People love to receive gifts, even small ones.

By bringing a large cup of coffee to your meeting, you will instantly be received with a smile. The person will appreciate the hot beverage because he is busy and probably needs the caffeine boost no matter what time of day it is. More importantly, he will instantly know you are a person of your word. Be sure to bring the cream, sugar, and stir stick, too.

I brought along a coffee to the meeting I had at Alliance Atlantis. It went great, because the person I met with was an incredible guy. He was young and energetic with an undeniable passion for television.

Did I end up working for the company? No. However, my coffee-powered meeting with him must have stuck in his mind, because years later he hired me.

The Meeting

The coffee meetings I have had have always gone longer than the 15 minutes I requested. They always end up being 30 to 60 minutes. This is because people love to talk about themselves and share their stories and wisdom.

In Chapter 10, "Listen Better. Remember More," I'll share important ways to improve your listening skills. For now, I'll say that you must listen carefully during the meeting. Look her in the eyes, smile, and nod. Genuinely enjoy the conversation and your time together. Ask a lot of open-ended questions. Think of yourself as an interviewer on a talk show. It is fine to talk a little about yourself. You want your business contact to get to know you and like you too, but be sure you are not doing the bulk of the talking.

When your meeting concludes, be sure to say thank you. If the moment is right, ask if there's anyone else you should speak with in the industry. Does your contact have any colleagues or peers that might be willing to share their wisdom with you?

As soon as you leave the person's office, sit down and take some notes. If you are walking distance from a coffee shop, treat yourself to a cup for a job well done. Regardless of where you are, be sure to start writing notes sooner than later.

Write down the time and date of the meeting, who it was with, and the company name. What did the person tell you? What did you learn about the industry? What did you learn about the individual? What are your next steps? Do you now have

some contacts to get in touch with, or are you supposed to follow up next week? Write down the details while they're fresh in your mind.

Follow-Up

When you return to your office or home, write an email to say thank you. You may wish to take it a step further and send a thank-you card as well.

If you didn't get a chance to ask for additional introductions during your meeting, be sure to mention this in your thank-you email. Promise that you will keep in touch.

Is there a promise that you made during your meeting? Did you reference an article or something that the contact was interested in learning more about? Include a link to the article in the email. Give the person something of value when you say thank you.

Your follow-up should be all of the following:

- **Appreciative**—Express your appreciation for the person giving you her valuable time and information.
- **Complimentary**—Tell her what you learned and why you admire her.
- **Valuable**—Provide a link to an article or topic you discussed—something she will enjoy reading.
- **Open ended**—Let her know that you will keep in touch, and you hope she will do the same.

Don't forget to include a request for an introduction to anyone else in the industry that she feels you should meet. These introductions are important!

Here is an example:

> Dear Mrs. Smith,
>
> It was a pleasure meeting with you today. I sincerely appreciate you giving me your time in your busy schedule.
>
> I am so impressed that you began your career while you were still in high school. You have certainly inspired me to continue to follow my passion.
>
> I looked up the article I mentioned to you about the marketing program for company X. Here is the link if you wish to review it: http://...
>
> If you can think of anyone else I should meet in the industry, I would appreciate the introduction please.

I enjoyed meeting with you today. I am grateful that you took the time to share so much of your wisdom about the industry. Your experiences and knowledge are impressive!

I hope that we can keep in touch. Please let me know if I can be of assistance to you in any way.

Thank you for your time,

Bill Jones

Now is a good time to connect on LinkedIn. LinkedIn can be an extremely valuable tool in your networking efforts, so use it wisely. If you have an opportunity to connect with someone there, do it.

Don't just send a generic request to add this person to your network. Write a short, personal message instead. Be sure your LinkedIn profile is up to snuff before doing this. I'll write more about using the popular business social network in Chapter 4, "Grow Your Network Before You Need It: LinkedIn."

Laid Off and Networking

As my job at the publicity company was coming to a close, I was asking close friends and family where I should turn next. Working for a small performing arts publicity company was fun, and I really enjoyed interacting with people in the entertainment industry.

My Mum and her partner, Bob, were both long-time theater ticket subscribers for Mirvish Productions, Canada's largest theater producers. When we sat down one night over dinner and the conversation turned to my work predicament, they suggested that I get in touch with someone there.

If you can name a Broadway musical that has opened in Toronto, Mirvish has probably produced it. I made the call and set up a meeting. And yes, you can bet I brought a coffee.

Soon after the meeting I was called back to interview for a job. I was hired as the marketing manager for the Toronto production of *Hairspray*, the Broadway musical.

Note that you may not get hired as soon as you meet someone. It may take weeks or months of meetings before you find yourself employed again. Do not allow yourself to be discouraged. Networking usually takes time.

Being laid off is a terrible experience, but understand that the change will lead you to something new, and often something bigger and better. If you are laid off, don't

panic. Instead, take inventory of the situation. Use a notepad or journal to record your experiences and thoughts on the matter.

Ask yourself why you were laid off, and what you learned from both the job and the experience of being laid off. Write it down.

- Think about where you have come from. Where did your career begin, and where are you now? Jot this down.
- What do you want to do now? Take some notes about what the best steps are to get back on your feet. I bet it includes reaching out to members of your network.
- Picture where you want to be in five years. Write it down, and work backward through the steps needed to reach this goal.
- Now take a moment to export your LinkedIn connections and email address book. Print them out.
- Review who you know and what companies they work for. Are any of these companies places you want to work?
- Brainstorm other companies in your industry, and write down the ones you would love to work for. Check LinkedIn to see if you have connections at these companies. Ask for introductions.
- Contact your friends and family to see who they may know.
- Set up some informal interviews, and don't forget the coffee!

There is value in every relationship you have. Instead of being frustrated by not seeing the value right away, you should consider how you can bring value for members of your network. Networking is a two-way street. Focus on helping others, and good will come your way as a result. I am not speaking of karma here. However, you may see some similarities in how successful networking works.

One idea to help others is to take note of who is looking for work in your network. As you grow your contacts on LinkedIn, you may know the perfect person for a position. Be a connector, and introduce people so that they may help each other. Sure, you may be looking for a job too, but that shouldn't stop you from helping your network.

The New Kid in Town

When I moved to Nashville, I didn't know a soul. I knew that relying on career websites would probably not amount to much in the way of my career. Instead, I spent the bulk of my time researching the companies I wanted to work for and the events where I could meet the people to make it happen.

The Nashville chapter of the American Marketing Association (NAMA) seemed to be a perfect place for me to get my toes wet and meet the local marketing community. Most larger cities have organizations and related groups dedicated to your industry. I reviewed the NAMA site and noted the president, Karen Stone.

I emailed Karen to ask her a little more about NAMA. She promptly replied and invited me to their seasonal social hour. I attended with high hopes of meeting other marketing professionals so I could grow my network and find employment.

Networking is work, but it is rewarding work. It should also be enjoyable. Even if you consider yourself an introvert, don't fret. Be comfortable by researching the events, people, and companies you plan to meet with.

Know your story. What's your elevator pitch? If you are fearful of meeting people, rehearse your brief story. Think about your personal pitch—not your business pitch, but your personal story. What is it that you want me to know about you? We only have a moment in the elevator. What are you going to tell me?

I wanted people to know that I was an experienced marketing professional who had recently relocated with my family to Nashville. I wanted to meet with as many people as I could to learn about Nashville's entertainment, media, and new media marketing industries.

It may sound silly, and it will certainly feel silly, but practice your elevator pitch in front of your bathroom mirror. I recommend waiting until you are home alone, so your roommate or family do not become concerned with your sanity as they hear you talking to yourself.

In addition to practicing your pitch, be sure to think about a few questions to ask others. Some good questions are

- What brings you to this event?
- What do you do for a living? What made you choose this career?
- Are you from _____ originally? If not, where are you from? What brought you to _____?
- Do you have family here? What does your partner do?

Avoid questions that are too personal, but ask questions of the people you meet. This is a crucial part of networking. I understand if you are shy, but even shy people need to go on dates and job interviews, right?

I met a lot of great people during the NAMA event. Karen was an incredibly gracious host who went out of her way to introduce me to many people in the room. I will always be thankful for her kindness. After the event, I emailed Karen to set up a meeting to further discuss the marketing industry in Nashville.

She kindly took me up on my offer. I brought the coffee, of course. As our meeting came to a close, I asked her for any recommendations for other people I should meet in town.

In a moment of excitement to help me further, Karen pulled out a pen and piece of paper and began to jot down names of people she thought I should meet. One of those people was Hannah Paramore, president of a local new marketing agency.

I contacted Hannah after my meeting with Karen. Hannah invited me into her office to meet her in person. What I learned quickly about moving to Nashville is how warm and hospitable people are.

After chatting with Hannah for some time, she suggested I meet her friend, Clint Smith, who is cofounder of the popular email marketing company Emma. Clint agreed to meet with me the same day. In fact, it all happened in a heartbeat.

Hannah set up my meeting with Clint. She printed an interview from the paper about Emma, so I could read it on my way to the meeting. I knew nothing about Emma, but I got a little acquainted as I read the article at red lights and in the parking lot at Emma just 15 minutes later.

At this time, like many Nashville start-ups, Emma was in a house. When I arrived, I walked up the front porch steps and through the screen door into the front room of the office. A group of friendly faces greeted me, all sitting behind Apple computers.

I had researched the events I needed to attend in Nashville. I met Karen at an event, and she introduced me to Hannah, who introduced me to Clint. This is the true power of networking. You must get offline after researching and attend the events where the people are. Networking works best in person, so get out there and do it.

Back at Emma, it was nearly Beer Thirty. Each Friday at 4:30 the company graciously supplied its staff with some cold beer and snacks. Having worked for larger, more traditional companies, this was a refreshing taste of how small companies treat their employees.

Clint and I met, and he introduced me to some of the staff. I thoroughly enjoyed my time speaking with Clint. He is a smart, charismatic, and funny gentleman. I had to remind myself that I was there to meet him and learn about Emma, rather than apply for a position. However, the thought of working for Emma certainly came to my mind. I enjoyed the creative, youthful approach to an otherwise old technology—email.

That evening I wrote thank-you emails to Hannah and Clint. Clint replied that he would like me to meet his chief technology officer, Marcus Whitney. My meeting with Marcus would shape the future of my career and life in Nashville.

Are you following along at this point? Do you see what has happened thus far?

1. I researched organizations and people in Nashville.

2. I cold-called Karen Stone, the president of NAMA.

3. Karen met with me and introduced me to Hannah Paramore.

4. Hannah introduced me to Clint Smith, cofounder of Emma.

5. Clint introduced me to Marcus Whitney, Emma's CTO.

Not only was I networking well, but the people I met were doing so as well. The people I was meeting were going out of their way to help me by introducing me to other people in their networks. I want to stress that we must always be thinking about how to help others as we grow our networks.

I exchanged emails with Marcus, and we arranged to meet for a coffee (my treat, of course). We hit it off instantly. I enjoyed his energy and great spirit about technology and life in Nashville. He was also a convert from the north, being from Brooklyn, New York.

Marcus and I began discussing an idea to create an event to celebrate technology in Nashville. I will share the details of the event and how you can create your own in Chapter 9, "If You Build It, They Will Come: Organizing Events." What I didn't realize was that Marcus was feeling me out for a job with Emma.

Shortly after meeting Marcus, Clint emailed me to invite me back to Emma for a chat. A job as new media specialist followed soon after.

My first job came to me in Nashville from actively attending events and meeting people. The meetings I described that led to employment were far from the only ones. I met with senior people in print, television, and other related marketing fields.

Networking can be exhausting; I'll be the first to admit it. As you'll recall, I was living at my in-law's home in Jackson, Tennessee. This meant that I had to drive two hours to Nashville each time I had meetings lined up or an event to attend. I followed this up with two hours back to Jackson after spending the day growing my network.

What are you doing to grow your network? What are you prepared to do?

Review your New Networking spreadsheet. It's time to invite someone for a coffee. Better yet, why don't you bring the coffee to your contact instead?

Did buying someone a coffee work for you? I encourage you to share your story at New-Networking.com.

3

Your Home on the Web Needs More Than a Welcome Mat

She's going to check you out. At least that's what you hope she does after meeting you at a networking event or conference. He's going to want to learn a little more about you after a short correspondence on Twitter. He'll look at your brief bio, and he'll likely click a link if you include one. Where will it lead?

In Chapter 11, "Business Cards That Rock and When to Use Them," I'll write more about what works and what doesn't for business cards. However, this chapter is about where that card leads a person. If your card doesn't have information on how I can learn more about you, it defeats the purpose.

In Chapter 1, "Do Your Homework," I wrote about researching attendees before an event. If I see that you're attending an event, I hope you have a presence online so I can learn more about why I want to meet you.

You need to own your domain. Stop reading this right now and visit a reputable hosting company to purchase your personal domain. I recommend Hosting.com, NetworkSolutions.com, or GoDaddy.com. Try to find yourname.com as your URL. If it's unavailable, you can purchase yourname.me or include a middle initial.

You need your own URL, so you can give people you meet a way to learn more about you. Understand that the URL is not one that will necessarily replace your own business site or the company where you work, but it will complement it.

I'll explain how you'll use this personal URL to promote your social profiles like Twitter, Facebook, and LinkedIn.

If you're attending a conference or event on behalf of a client or employer, it's wise not to hand out your own business cards. You're there to represent the firm, not yourself. However, it's not uncommon to meet someone you don't have a business opportunity with—someone you simply want to get to know better. In this case, handing the individual a personal card is okay.

If you're between jobs or a student about to embark on your career, you especially need to have a home on the web. Buy your domain name and redirect where you want a person to go to learn more about you.

About.me

About.me is a free service that easily lets you configure a personal landing page, also known as a *splash page*. I love About.me because it's simple to design a great-looking page quickly. It also includes a small analytics dashboard that shows you how people interact with your content and where they're visiting the page from. Figures 3.1 and 3.2 show some cool example pages.

Figure 3.1   *Jeffrey Sass About.me page: http://about.me/sass.*

Figure 3.2   *Baratunde Thurston About.me page: http://about.me/baratunde.*

I recommend using your About.me page to share your social profiles. You should consider using it to link to Twitter, Facebook, Pinterest, LinkedIn, your blog, your own company site, or your employer's site. Provide a bio so that visitors can learn more about you.

Flavors.me

An alternative to About.me is Flavors.me, owned by Moo.com.

Flavors.me has better design capabilities than About.me (see Figures 3.3 and 3.4). It's still easy to use and similar to About.me. The basic version is free and provides you with everything you need to create a splash page, including some basic analytics to monitor traffic in real time. Unlike About.me, if you pay for Flavors.me (approximately $20/year), you receive some bonus options worth considering.

Figure 3.3   *Amber MacArthur Flavors.me page: http://flavors.me/ambermac.*

Figure 3.4   *Nan Palmero Flavors.me page: http://flavors.me/nanpalmero*

The benefit of a paid subscription for Flavors.me is the option of using a custom domain. Rather than someone entering www.johnsmith.com and the site being redirected to flavors.me/johnsmith, the URL will remain as www.johnsmith.com, which looks much more professional.

A paid subscription also comes with an analytics package so you can track clicks to your page, similar to About.me.

About.me and Flavors.me are the fastest and easiest options to design your own social landing page. Each allows even a novice designer to create something visually appealing. Be sure to include the links to your social profiles, business, and other relevant links. Professional designers may prefer the paid version of Flavors. me because of its more advanced design options and templates.

After you've set up your splash page, you need to redirect your domain to the page. Most web hosting services should be able to help you on this common item. If you can't see how to do it, you may find your answer on your host's FAQ or support forums. If all else fails, you can always pick up the phone and call the host directly.

Ideally, you want to use a custom domain name rather than a redirect. This is available in the paid version of Flavors.me.

Blogging

A personal splash landing page like the ones outlined earlier will certainly do the trick when pointing people to your online home. However, if you really want to impress your new contacts, blogging is a great option.

Originally, a blog was a weblog made for people to share their thoughts on an array of topics from personal to business-related items in an online journaling style. The beauty of blogging regularly is that you can show the world who you are while teaching yourself about a topic. You may even learn something about yourself.

Before I moved to Nashville, Tennessee, I created a blog called "New Media Nashville." By writing about the new media industry in the city I would soon call my home, I learned about the companies and different people I wanted to meet. "New Media Nashville" was a research project on top of a personal branding initiative.

Whenever I'm asked to speak to students, I stress that they should be blogging. They should openly write and share what they're learning about their industries. By establishing themselves online, they're showing future employers that they're dedicated and passionate about their career path. As a recruiter, I would be impressed to find a candidate with a blog dedicated to the area of focus.

Begin by searching for topics of interest using Google or StumbleUpon. Tablet users should check out apps like Zite and Flipboard to discover great content. Share the good content that you find, and use your blog to add your own commentary.

Tumblr

Tumblr is a free service that offers a simple form of blogging. Tumblr users call this *Tumblelogging*. It's best used to share different forms of media such as videos, images, audio, and text. Tumblr blog posts are usually shorter than typical blogs as far as text content goes. However, they're usually filled with rich visual content.

Tumblr comes with hundreds of free themes that cover an array of stylish templates. You'll also find paid themes that may be more suitable for the design you're seeking. You can search them at www.tumblr.com/themes.

Tumblr also introduces you to a strong community, which a splash page can't do. Using Tumblr, you can search and share content you like from other users. Networking happens best when you're doing it with people with similar interests. Be sure to frequently share other content from other people's Tumblr accounts. You can share Tumblr posts you like by pressing the heart-shaped Like button or arrows to reblog the post on your own Tumblr blog.

Remember that Tumblr leans more toward the arts and creatives, so consider this in determining whether it is where you should plant your flag on the web.

Another great thing with Tumblr is that you can use a custom domain. Therefore, johnsmith.tumblr.com will appear as johnsmith.com, which looks more professional.

 Note

Your URL can only go to one site. Choose to point it to your splash page, where you promote all your social profiles and links to your blog or directly to your blog.

At this point you can consider between having a splash page using About.me or Flavors.me or a quick and design-friendly blog on Tumblr. If you want to take this a step further, you should consider a more extensive blog using WordPress or Blogger.

Blogger

Blogger.com is a free blogging service provided by Google. The biggest benefit of using Blogger is that Google owns it, which means it's a stable platform and host.

Google makes blogging quite simple using its easy interface. You can set up a blog within minutes from your free Gmail account. Its dashboard provides you with a basic overview of statistics to show you the number of views to your blog.

A basic Blogger blog has a domain like johnsmith.blogspot.com. If you choose to use Blogger, I recommend that you use a custom domain like I previously explained. It looks more professional to have yourname.com.

You can choose from custom templates to customize your blog so it's more fitting for your needs.

You can write posts (articles) and schedule them to publish on your blog in the future. This way you can rest easy knowing you have content scheduled.

A common term in blogging is *tags*. We use tags to help visitors and search engines find our posts by associating them with a handful of words that best describe the content. For example, if I write a blog post about blogging tips, I will use *blogging* and *tips* as tags for the post. You'll find the use of tags across all blogging platforms. However, Google calls them *labels*. Keep in mind that they may have different names, but they work the same way.

Blogger is a great free service for a novice with little technical know-how. I started blogging with Blogger many years ago. Over time I realized that if I wanted a blog with better options and more customization, I would need to move on to WordPress. Luckily, there are tools available to export your Blogger blog to a WordPress blog. However, you may decide to skip Blogger and save yourself the transferring headache later.

WordPress

Most experienced bloggers or web professionals will agree that WordPress is the best way to go for your blog.

There are three options to choose from when proceeding with WordPress:

1. **WordPress.com, a free option to host your blog**—If you choose the free version, you will have a domain like johnsmith.wordpress.com. I recommend avoiding this, because it is more professional to use your own domain, like johnsmith.com.

    The free version is also ad supported, so your blog will have advertisements that are out of your control.

2. **The paid version of WordPress.com**—This will give you the option to use a custom domain, like johnsmith.com. The paid version also removes ads and gives you more options, including 10GB space upgrade, no advertisements, custom design, and VideoPress (video hosting).

Note

3. **The self-hosted WordPress.org**—This is free to download and install,
   but you need to pay hosting fees associated with running the blog. This
   is the option I suggest you proceed with, because it is the most customizable with different templates (designs) and plug-ins (functionality).
   However, it does take some knowledge of hosting and FTP.

FTP stands for File Transfer Protocol. When you manage the hosting of your blog
or website, you have the ability to use FTP software. The advantage of FTP is that
you are in full control of the physical files on your site. You can easily upload,
download, or transfer files to new directories and back them up regularly.

The good news is many decent hosting services now come with WordPress already
installed. I recommend that you use the same service that you will use to purchase
your domain. For example, if you use Hosting.com to buy your domain, use that
company for your hosting, too. Good hosting services offer technical support so
you can get the help you need to get your blog up and running. I've always been
impressed with the support at GoDaddy.com and Hosting.com., but there are
plenty of other great hosts.

Third-party plug-ins will make your blog that much better, too. *Plug-ins* are tiny
programs made to enhance the blogger's experience within WordPress and the
reader experience on the blog. There are thousands of plug-ins to choose from,
some better than others. The plug-ins can be found in a massive directory at
WordPress.org/extend/plugins/.

 Tip

Always read the ratings and check the reviews before installing a plug-in.
You should also see when it was last updated to be sure it is being maintained as new versions of WordPress become available.

Once your WordPress blog is available and you are logged in, you need to choose
a template. Like Tumblr, there are many options to get an incredible template. You
can find free templates across the Web or within WordPress itself. You can also
pay for a template that is ready to go. If you prefer, you can spend more money
and hire a WordPress developer to create a template that is truly original.

I know that every new blogger enters with great enthusiasm. They write feverishly, knocking out seven posts (articles) a week. Everything is going gangbusters, but then it happens. The seven posts slow down to five, the five to three, three becomes one, and worse, posts become biweekly or monthly. Blogger fatigue is real, so keep this in mind.

It's best to write the blog for a month or two before making it live. This way you can get into a groove and determine the optimal pace you want to publish content. If your blog posts are not time sensitive, it's wise to write some future posts so they can be scheduled on your editorial calendar.

Editorial Calendar

One of the best WordPress plug-ins is Editorial Calendar by Stresslimit. This plug-in creates a calendar view of the weeks and months ahead, so you can plan which posts will be published when. I love that you can interact directly with the calendar. By clicking on a date, you can create a draft post (see Figure 3.5). You can also pick up a post on a certain date and drag and drop it to another date if you feel you need to reschedule something. See http://wordpress.org/extend/plugins/editorial-calendar/.

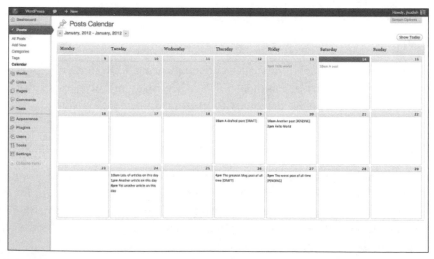

Figure 3.5   *Editorial Calendar for WordPress by Stresslimit and Zack Grossbart: http://stresslimitdesign.com/editorial-calendar-plugin.*

Whether you choose Tumblr, Blogger, or WordPress, planning ahead in blogging is a good way to relieve the stress that can sometimes occur when you know you need to be writing. A dormant blog can reflect poorly on you or your business, so consider your commitment to keeping it consistent.

Commenting

By becoming a blogger, you join a massive community of other Web content producers. By the end of 2011, there were approximately 181 million blogs around the world.[2] On WordPress.com alone, there are about 500,000 new posts and 400,000 new comments on an average day.[3]

Commenting is an important way to interact with your readers and to grow your community. Remember that networking is all about connecting with people who have similar interests. Writing a blog about a topic that is helpful and relevant to your readers will encourage comments, and new relationships will come from these interactions.

There are several decent options when it comes to managing comments on your blog. WordPress has its own built-in commenting system. Facebook also can be used to power your comments. It's a good option, but it's restrictive to Facebook users. Facebook comments uses its popular Facebook Connect, which developers use to connect Facebook to just about any site, so visitors can easily like, share, and comment on content.

Some other blog commenting services include Livefyre, IntenseDebate, and Disqus. Don't forget that you can also use the default commenting systems that WordPress and Blogger provide.

Livefyre

Livefyre is another option to manage your commenting. I like that Livefyre allows users to tag one another in comments. This means that you'll be alerted automatically should someone mention you (with a tag) in a comment.

IntenseDebate

IntenseDebate is a commenting system created by Auttomatic, the same people who created WordPress. One big plus of IntenseDebate is its point system for rating the best comments. The comments that gain the most points from visitors rise to the top below your blog post, becoming the first ones seen. This can add a little competition between the commenters.

I like the way IntenseDebate can be installed to work with Tumblr, Blogger, WordPress, and other blog platforms. This makes it an easy option for you to consider as a third-party host of your comments. It also works with Twitter and Facebook should someone choose to leave a comment without an IntenseDebate profile.

Disqus

My personal favorite third-party commenting service is Disqus. I've been using Disqus on several blogs for the past few years. I'm consistently impressed with the frequency of updates to Disqus's service to meet the changing needs of bloggers and their commenters.

Disqus features I like include:

- **In-line email moderation**—You get an email to let you know when a comment has been left. You can reply to the comment via your email or choose to approve (if you select comments to be moderated first) or delete it.
- **Social logins**—Your commenter can log in to leave a comment using Facebook, Twitter, Google Plus, or Disqus.
- **Export options**—You can export your comments to back them up. Like everything we produce online, it's wise to back up your content frequently.

When it comes down to it, you need to choose the comment service that works best for your needs. You may decide to stick with native commenting that comes installed with Tumblr, WordPress, or Blogger, and that's fine. However, third-party services tend to do a better job at combating spam and provide additional benefits such as comment voting, tagging, and improved moderations. Livefyre, IntenseDebate, and Disqus all have great features, so take a look at each service and decide which will serve you best.

If a person takes the time to leave you a comment, you should take the time to respond. This may be simply liking the comment, sending a brief thank-you message, or even better, actually responding to the comment. How can you continue the conversation? Can you ask the commenter a question related to his comment? Perhaps you can use this opportunity to introduce the commenter to another commenter who can provide additional insight.

Remember that by interacting and providing additional advice to your commenters, you strengthen your relationships. This is an important part of networking online through blogging. Never ignore your community.

Encourage conversation and provide ways to do so to keep the comments flowing.

Blogger Tips

Based on personal experience, I've come up with some tips to make your blogging experience easier and more worthwhile.

Know Why

With a pen and paper, jot down the reasons you think you should start a blog. What do you hope to achieve with it?

Chris Brogan (www.chrisbrogan.com), a New York Times best-selling author and popular blogger, has a blog to share his thoughts, promote his business, and build his network. He does this by writing about people he meets who inspire him, using social media marketing, and being proactive in his comments.

Why do you want to start a blog? What do you want to write about? Is there a specific topic you can write about frequently? What common questions do you receive about your line of work? Would the answers make great blog posts? Stop now and grab your notebook. Spend at least 15 minutes answering these questions and brainstorming about your potential blog.

Be able to clearly define why you plan to start your blog. Share your thoughts with the New Networking community at www.new-networking.com. Once your blog is live, share it with us here.

Know Your Audience

Who do you want to read your blog? Is it potential employers? Is it industry peers? Is it your customers or potential customers? Here are three good examples:

1. Author and Explore Conference planner Jason Falls writes "Social Media Explorer" at www.socialmediaexplorer.com, a site dedicated to the business of social media. His readers are business people who have an interest in learning about developing strong social media strategies. It's clear he understands who he's writing for.

2. Marcus Sheridan, CEO of River Pools & Spas, transformed his company when the economy took a turn for the worse. His clever blog posts drive traffic to his business and in turn increase sales. Do a Google search for "best pool builders in Virginia," and the blog post you find has earned $150,000 in sales.[4]

3. Ronni Bennett writes "Times Goes By" at www.timegoesby.net. She leads a team of writers who focus on topics about technology and issues for people in the later years in life. I love the way she coined the term *elder bloggers*.

All three examples are very different blogs, but each is dedicated to specific topics for specific audiences. Who is your audience? Who do you hope to reach?

Stick to Your Schedule

Consistency is key. Your readers will come to expect posts from you on a regular basis, so determine the best frequency for you. I mentioned earlier that you may begin writing five posts a week but eventually slip to one. It's okay to write one post a week, but don't drop below that number.

Consider selecting the days you'll write a blog post, such as Tuesdays and Fridays. Don't forget to use the Editorial Calendar WordPress plug-in. By populating the calendar, you can have an overview of the weeks ahead to help you stick to your schedule.

Both Tumblr and Blogger also include the option to schedule your posts. You can use a spreadsheet, your calendar software, or even an old-school paper calendar to jot down which posts you have scheduled when.

Having an editorial calendar is a wonderful way to have an overview of what posts you have planned for the future. Don't be overwhelmed by this. You don't need to have posts written months in advance, but being able to see what is scheduled in the next few weeks can be helpful when planning.

Encourage Conversation

A great way to stir conversation is to ask a question at the end of your post. Ask your readers to leave a comment with their opinion. Opinionated posts are a great way to get the discussion going. You can also be a little controversial, but remember that what you post online will remain. Think carefully before you publish the blog post. If the content is questionable, you would be wise to allow your associate, friend, or family member to review it for her opinion first.

Consider Moderation

The choice is yours to allow comments at all, automatically approve all comments, or hold them for moderation. Most blogs allow comments, but they do so in different ways. Unfortunately, troublemakers, or *trolls* as they are commonly known online, exist. Trolls intentionally leave nasty comments. More on trolls in a moment.

If you own an email account (which I know you do), you're familiar with spam. Nobody likes spam except spammers. Unfortunately, blog commenting sections are targets to spammers. It's important to stay on top of the problems like trolls and spammers.

If you have blog comments set to moderation, you're notified when a comment is left. You have the option to either approve the comment or reject and delete it. This occurs instantly once you've made the decision about the comment. Finally, you can mark the comment as spam, which alerts your commenting host to reject future comments from the account.

Moderating comments is fine, but you need to approve them quickly. Unless you're blogging about a controversial topic, I recommend allowing all comments. Be sure to review them as they're left, though, so you can remove any spam comments that slip through the cracks.

I allow negative comments if they're tasteful. Your readers will likely come to your defense should negativity occur. Always try to review comments in a timely manner. Reply if you can as well, so the commenter knows she's being heard.

On some corporate blogs, you can find a commenting policy in place. This protects you should you decide to delete comments you don't approve of. It can also inform the commenter as to what is acceptable. For example, if your blog is a family-friendly blog, you should restrict inappropriate language. Keep in mind that the more you police your comments, the less comments you'll receive.

Finally, don't feed the trolls. Trolls are the bullies of commenting sections. They're people who intentionally leave hurtful or abusive comments. I recommend removing these types of comments if they are abusive or don't meet your commenting policy. All commenting systems have an option to ban or blacklist a user.

Let your community interact and add their thoughts about what you've written. Don't feel that you must reply to every comment, but understand that interacting is important in comments.

Be Yourself

If you're writing a personal blog, let your personality shine through. Don't get stuck in formalities. This isn't a research paper. It's a conversation starter.

If your blog is intended for your personal business or for the company you work for, the same rule applies. Nobody likes to read corporate tongue. Press releases have their place, but your blog should not be one of them. Instead, take your press release content and rewrite it in a personal way. What milestone is your company celebrating? Share your true story about how you reached the goal.

Be honest, sincere, and authentic. We hear the word *authentic* so often in social media, with good reason. Write from the heart. You'll find that your content gets shared and receives comments more often this way.

Use Social Sharing

I have reserved chapters in this book to social networking sites like LinkedIn, Twitter, and Facebook. What you need to know now as you are considering blogging is how to make your content easily sharable.

Each blog service you use comes with some form of social sharing option. If the option is not included for a particular social network, you'll probably be able to find the code to set it up yourself relatively easily. Go to your favorite social networking site and search for *buttons* or *goodies* to find out how to add them.

Plenty of great WordPress plug-ins will add the essential Twitter retweet, Facebook like, Google +1, Reddit, and LinkedIn share options to each of your posts. A personal favorite is Slick Social Share Buttons, found at http://wordpress.org/extend/plugins/slick-social-share-buttons/. Review who you're writing for, and consider the best options for them. For example, if you're writing primarily to a female audience about a visual topic like home decor or fashion or to a heavy social media crowd, you'll definitely want to include Pinterest. You'll find more plug-ins at http://wordpress.org/extend/plugins/.

If you write about specific industry- or business-related topics, you'll want to be sure LinkedIn is an option for sharing. Consider the types of people who use social networking sites like LinkedIn, Pinterest, and Reddit. If your blog content will be enjoyed by these users, be sure to give them an easy way to share it.

A Picture Tells a Thousand Words

Do your best to include an image in each blog post because images help tell the story. They also make your content more visually pleasing. In addition to this, images help your stories spread.

If I like your blog post on Facebook, your image will be included in my timeline. This increases the chance of my friends clicking the item to learn more about it. If I pin your blog post to one of my boards on Pinterest, an image is necessary.

 Caution

Consider the license on the image you choose in your blog post. It's wrong to steal someone's photo or illustration and just post it in your blog post. Instead, consider using your own photography, use free or paid stock photography, or use Flickr to search its Creative Commons section.

There are several different levels of Creative Commons licenses, so choose carefully. The last thing you want is to be accused of stealing someone's work. You will learn more about Creative Commons licensing in Chapter 8.

Increase Traffic with Search Engine Optimization

Optimizing your content for search engines is a good way to increase traffic to your blog. The topic of search engine optimization (SEO) is too massive to cover in this book. I encourage you to subscribe to Christopher S. Penn's blog, "Awaken Your Superhero," at www.christopherspenn.com/. Chris is knowledgeable when it comes to SEO and online marketing in general.

Here are two suggestions to improve your SEO performance:

1. **Use Google's Keyword tool**—This is a tool to optimize your advertisements for Google. However, the information learned is still relevant for writing effective copy online. Search variations of the terms you're writing about. For example, if you own a restaurant and you're writing a post about a new vegetarian lasagna, you may search for *vegetarian lasagna*, *vegetable lasagna*, and *lasagna for vegetarians*. Using Google's Keyword tool, you can determine which words and phrases are searched for most frequently. This can help you use language that is most likely to be searched for.

2. **Use WordPress SEO plug-in**—I really like the WordPress SEO plug-in by Yoast, found at http://wordpress.org/extend/plugins/wordpress-seo/. The free plug-in adds a section below your blog post to optimize your content. The clever plug-in scans the text in your post and gives you a short report. You can add additional meta content that will increase the likeliness of your content being found. You can find other SEO-related WordPress plug-ins in the WordPress directory at http://wordpress.org/extend/plugins/search.php?q=seo. Be sure to read the most recent reviews before installing.

It's important to consider the rules of SEO. You need to be sure you're always practicing "white hat" techniques that won't get your blog penalized by Google and other search engines. I recommend that you visit Google's Webmaster Tools section of their site. There you will find the Search Engine Optimization Starter Guide to learn more.

 Note

White Hat is a term given for approved forms of optimization. Grey Hat means the technique may be questionable, and Black Hat is against search engine policies. It's best to stick with "white hat" techniques.

Remember that it's your content that is most important. Write high-quality, engaging, original content, and people will find you. If your blog posts provide readers with insight and knowledge, you'll be helping them.

Not only will your blog act as an incredibly rewarding place to grow your network, but you'll become more knowledgeable as you research and write about the topics your customers and industry peers are interested in.

Darren Rowse began blogging in 2002. In 2004, he created ProBlogger.net, a blog dedicated to the topic of blogging for money. Since then, he has added well over 3,500 articles, tips, tutorials, and case studies. Darren's Facebook page for ProBloggers has more than 40,000 members, and his Twitter account has over 176,000 followers. You can follow his community at Problogger.com.

Darren is a great example of someone who found a topic he is passionate about and turned it into a full-time blog and business. His frequent readers and commenters were also likely the first people to purchase his book, *ProBlogger's Guide to Your First Week of Blogging.* They also became advocates for it.

Don't abuse the trust of your readers by shamelessly plugging yourself, your services, or your products. Instead, use it to sell me on why you are someone I should meet or do business with.

Your home on the Web needs more than a welcome mat. It needs to include information and ways to connect with you. Use it to share your Twitter account, Facebook page, Google+, LinkedIn profile, and blog if you decide to go that route.

I want to see what you come up with, too. I am @davedelaney on Twitter. Say hello and send me a link to your home on the Web. I look forward to learning more about you.

Endnotes

1. http://en.wordpress.com/stats/

2. http://blog.nielsen.com/nielsenwire/online_mobile/buzz-in-the-blogosphere-millions-more-bloggers-and-blog-readers/

3. http://en.wordpress.com/stats/

4. www.prnewsonline.com/free/The-Lion-in-the-Pool-Marcus-Sheridan-Demystifies-Content-Marketing_16923.html

4

Grow Your Network Before You Need It: LinkedIn

There are approximately 3.4 million students graduating from college this year in the United States alone.[1] That is 3.4 million people seeking to begin their professional careers. Combine this group with the 12 million unemployed in this country,[2] and you can understand how competitive the job market is. In this chapter I share tips and advice on using LinkedIn to jump-start your career, get back on your feet, or grow your business.

LinkedIn is by far the number-one "professional" social networking site. Members use LinkedIn to share their professional profiles, network with industry peers, promote their work, create and join groups on many topics, and grow their networks.

The unemployed, recent graduates, or anyone seeking a career change can use LinkedIn to find new job openings and events and connect with peers who may lead them to their next position. Businesses also use LinkedIn to promote themselves and their open positions, network with other businesses, and showcase their products, services, and recommendations from their clients.

More than 150 million international members from 170 industries are on LinkedIn.[3] Competitors have come along to battle the professional social network, but nothing has come close to the success that LinkedIn continues to have.

With more than two million companies with LinkedIn pages and one million LinkedIn groups,[4] it's essential that you have your personal profile up to date and that you're actively growing your network on the best social network for business.

Creating Your Profile

Begin by creating your personal profile on LinkedIn. Follow the simple steps to get started by adding your employment history, education, and professional bio. Did you receive awards or reach special milestones in your school, community, personal business, or the company where you work? Be sure to add them to your bio.

When writing your bio, remember that LinkedIn is the professional social network. Keep things clean and appropriate to impress potential employers, employees, sales leads, and other business promotional partners.

Use a pleasant headshot, preferably one of you alone. Avoid poor crop jobs if you are removing someone from your photo. It looks strange to see a photo of someone with a random hand on his shoulder. Also, be sure you are smiling in the photo and dressed professionally. Would you hire yourself based on your photo? Would you do business with the person in the photo?

No professional work experience yet? No problem. Include your college and extracurricular activities. The fact that you are at college probably means you have had to work a part-time or full-time job. The job may not fit your dream career destination, but you probably performed tasks that will be related to your ideal job. For example, a restaurant server can include these skills: expeditious problem solver, punctual staff member, observant people person, creative problem solver, dedicated team member.

Add your areas of expertise and specialties. These will automatically be associated with your profile when it's revealed to your connections requesting endorsements. I'll elaborate on endorsements later in this chapter.

Upon completing your LinkedIn profile, be sure to review it for grammatical and spelling errors. Be honest about the information you provide. Your mom was right: Honesty is the best policy. Manners matter too, but I digress.

I spoke in Chapter 3, "Your Home on the Web Needs More Than a Welcome Mat," about the importance of search engine optimization (SEO) on your blog content. The same is true on your LinkedIn profile. Be sure to use keywords and terms specific to the industry you want to reach. There is no LinkedIn plug-in that will help you with this, so I recommend turning to Google's Contextual Targeting tool.

Using Google's Contextual Targeting Tool

You are probably wondering what advertising on Google has to do with LinkedIn. Allow me to explain. SEO is a widely recognized way to best optimize your content to appear in search engines. The same applies to LinkedIn search. If a job recruiter is searching your city for candidates, you'll want your profile to rise to the top of the search results. Using Google's Contextual Targeting Tool, you'll learn how best to write your profile, so you include multiple keywords and terms that people are searching for.

Visit adwords.google.com and sign in with a free Gmail account. Select Contextual Targeting Tool under the Tools and Analysis tab to get started.

Let's say you're a financial planner. You search for *financial planning and investment*. The Contextual Targeting tool gives you additional, related terms associated with your search, including *financial planning magazine*, *financial planning process*, *financial planning firms*, *family financial planning*, and *financial planning services*.

Consider how you can optimize your LinkedIn profile to include some of these terms. Don't go overboard with this process. It's important to include keywords to optimize your profile, but ultimately a human will be the one hiring you.

Did you know that 72% of resumes are never seen[5] because they're not optimized for applicant tracking software using keywords?

Optimizing your LinkedIn profile will improve the likeliness of your profile appearing in the top results of popular search engines and LinkedIn itself. There are no guarantees on this, but the more optimized your profile is, the better your chances.

 Tip

Be sure to customize your public profile. Instead of sticking with a profile with random characters, like linkedin.com/pub/83/67b/0000, choose your name instead, such as linkedin.com/in/janedoe. Do this by visiting linkedin.com/profile/public-profile-settings.

There's an App for That

Many people don't realize that LinkedIn lists great third-party and native applications to add to your profile to improve it. Table 4.1 is a list of suitable apps based on what your possible line of work may be.

Table 4.1   Applications for Your LinkedIn Profile

Line of Work	App	Description
Realtors	Real Estate Pro by Rofo	"Access your local real estate and office space market. Follow active brokers, agents, and professionals. Track new property listings and available spaces and stay informed of completed deals in your area."
Lawyers	Lawyer Ratings by LexisNexis Martindale-Hubbell	"Showcase your Martindale-Hubbell Peer Review Ratings and Client Review Ratings to further validate your stated credentials and help you make the right connections."
	Legal Updates by JD Supra	"Get legal news that matters to you and your business. (Lawyers, upload your articles and other content. Be found for your expertise on LinkedIn.)"
Developers	GitHub by LinkedIn	"Showcase your GitHub projects on LinkedIn. Discover which of your LinkedIn Connections are most active on GitHub, and explore the projects they work on."
Designers	Portfolio Display by Behance	"Showcase your creative work in your LinkedIn Profile with the Creative Portfolio Display application. Free, easy to manage, and supports unlimited multimedia content."
Team Leaders	Projects and Teamspaces by Manymoon	"Manymoon makes it simple to get work done with your LinkedIn connections. Share and track unlimited tasks, projects, documents, and Google Apps—for free!"
	Box.net Files by Box.net	"Add the Box.net Files application to manage all your important files online. Box.net lets you share content on your profile and collaborate with friends and colleagues."

Line of Work	App	Description
Bloggers	WordPress by WordPress	"Connect your virtual lives with the WordPress LinkedIn application. With the WordPress app, you can sync your WordPress blog posts with your LinkedIn profile, keeping everyone you know in the know."
	Blog Link by SixApart	"With Blog Link, you can get the most of your LinkedIn relationships by connecting your blog to your LinkedIn profile. Blog Link helps you, and your professional network, stay connected."
Speakers	SlideShare Presentations by SlideShare Inc.	"SlideShare is the best way to share presentations on LinkedIn! You can upload and display your own presentations, check out presentations from your colleagues, and find experts within your network."

If none of these apps is appropriate for what you do, there are a few more to consider. See linkedin.com/apps. More apps are added from time to time, so refer back occasionally to see what's new.

- **Polls by LinkedIn**—"The Polls application allows you to collect actionable data from your connections and the professional audience on LinkedIn."

- **Events by LinkedIn**—"Find professional events, from conferences to local meetups, and make the right connections with other professionals at the event."

- **My Travel by TripIt, Inc.**—"See where your LinkedIn network is traveling and when you will be in the same city as your colleagues. Share your upcoming trips, current location, and travel stats with your network."

- **Reading List by Amazon**—"Extend your professional profile by sharing the books you're reading with other LinkedIn members. Find out what you should be reading by following updates from your connections, people in your field, or other LinkedIn members of professional interest to you."

- **E-Bookshelf by FT Press**—"Tap into the insights of the leading minds in business, E-Bookshelf by FT Press-essential reading for success. Read quick, concise business and career lessons from the top experts. Read the content you want, when you want and at a great value."

Start Connecting

Well, look at you. Don't you look lovely? You have your profile filled up. Your experiences, awards, and milestones are clearly listed. You've optimized your content to make the search engines happy. Good for you. Now it's time to begin connecting and building your LinkedIn contacts. This section is about finding connections and growing your network. It's a crucial part of making LinkedIn work for you.

From the navigation bar under Contacts, choose Add Connections. Select the email service provider that you use. You can select from Gmail, Outlook, Yahoo! Mail, Hotmail, or AOL. When you select one of these services, you need to give LinkedIn permission to access your contacts. Don't send invites to your entire list of contacts. Go through each contact and consider why you should invite that person to join you on LinkedIn. Is the person already a well-connected member of her community? Does he have a company you want to do business with? Do you actually know the person?

Follow the steps, and as LinkedIn writes, "Sit tight, your contacts are on the way." Once your contacts are available, you can tick the boxes next to the names of the people you want to invite to become a connection. LinkedIn sends them a message through its system. It's a good way to connect with a large number of people at one time.

A more time-consuming but better option is to manually invite people to connect with you. All you need is their email address. Instead of doing a bulk invitation, you can send individual requests. Always customize the generic message that LinkedIn provides. This shows that you truly want to connect with "me" and not just grow your database. Be personal about how you connect. Nobody likes generic messages.

 Tip

Did you know you can convert your LinkedIn profile into a resume? Visit resume.linkedinlabs.com to get started.

Are you a student? Take some time to think about who you can connect with to grow your LinkedIn connections. I've provided a list with some ideas. Consider each person's professional history. Don't just think of your parents as the people who raised you. Think of their professions. Everybody knows somebody, right?

- **Mom and Dad**—They are probably professionals with their own vast network of connections. They probably are your number-one fans, too.
- **Siblings**—How can your brothers and sisters help you? Do they work?

- **Summer jobs, part-time employment, and internships**—Can you request to be connected to any former managers or colleagues?

- **Classmates**—Have you worked on large projects with classmates? You will be graduating around the same time and will probably need each other to help jump-start your career.

- **Professors**—Connect with your favorite professors. Educators are well connected because they often come from the industry they teach in.

- **Fraternity brothers and sisters**—These connections are already loyal to you. Connect with them on LinkedIn before you graduate and go your separate ways.

- **Extended family**—Reach out and connect with your uncles, aunts, cousins, and grandparents.

- **Guest lecturers**—Consider requesting to connect with guest lecturers who visit your school. It's best to introduce yourself in person so they remember you first. If you asked them a question during the Q&A, they will recognize you.

- **Clergy**—Request to connect with your priest, rabbi, imam, or other religious leader.

 Tip

Refrain from sending LinkedIn connection requests to people you don't know or have never met. It's always best to meet the person before requesting to connect.

Once you have requested connections with people from your email contact list, LinkedIn will recommend that you request to connect with those who are not yet on LinkedIn. I did this when I joined LinkedIn in 2007. It still pleases me when a connection request I sent way back when is accepted so many years later. Some people are late to LinkedIn. That's fine, but the sooner you begin to use it, the better the rewards will be.

 Caution

Each LinkedIn account is allocated 3,000 invitations. Once you run out of invitations, you can contact LinkedIn to rectify this. The cap on invitations was made to prevent accidental or intentional abuse. You will know you're nearing your maximum number from a yellow warning box that appears above your invitation request.

Requesting Connections

When your connection request has been accepted, the person becomes a first-degree connection. First degree means that you're directly connected to the person on LinkedIn. A second-degree connection means a person is connected to you from one of your first-degree connections. Third-degree connections have two people between you and them.

You will see a *1st*, *2nd*, or *3rd* next to each profile name to let you know instantly if you're connected and to what degree. If you have a second- or third-degree connection to a person, LinkedIn reveals who in your contacts is connected to that person. You can see this on the right side of the person's profile page listed under "How You're Connected to X."

Here's a hypothetical example to better explain. My friend, Heather Smith (a first-degree connection), knows Mary Brown, who works with a large accounting firm. Mary will have a *2nd* next to her name, with Heather Smith listed as a first-degree connection on her profile page. Let's say I was seeking employment in accounting, I would contact Heather Smith for an introduction to Mary Brown through LinkedIn's messaging service. I would hope that my message to connect would lead to an introductory coffee meeting with Ms. Brown—just like I explained in Chapter 2, "It Starts with a Coffee."

A Basic LinkedIn account provides you with 5 InMail introduction messages. These are brief messages you can send to LinkedIn members you don't have a connection with. If you do not get a reply after seven days, LinkedIn will replace your InMail credit. A basic, free LinkedIn account user can also purchase up to ten InMail credits. You can learn more at: https://www.linkedin.com/static?key=about_inmail.

Promoting Your Profile

Don't take the time to build something without showing it off. You want people to connect with you on LinkedIn, so promote your profile everywhere.

- **Email Signature**—Add a link to your LinkedIn profile in every email you send.
- **Splash page**—Use your space on the Web to promote your profile. Add a link on your About.me or Flavors.me page.
- **Blog**—Add a badge on your blog so people can easily click through to your profile. Create yours at linkedin.com/profile/profile-badges.

- **Twitter**—Add a link in your Twitter bio section. This is especially good if you have no other site, blog, or splash page to include in your bio.
- **Facebook**—Share a link on your Facebook profile.

Taking Advantage of Endorsements

As you were carefully creating your profile, you will recall including your specialties, which quickly highlight your strengths to visitors of your profile. LinkedIn offers a unique way for you to endorse others and be endorsed based on the specialties you have outlined or ones others feel you excel at.

Under a user's profile, you will see an arrow next to Suggest Connections. Select Endorse Skills & Expertise from the drop-down. A blue window appears above the person's profile with specialties that you can select to endorse, or you can add your own.

By endorsing a contact, you achieve several things. You're sharing with your network that you recommend a person based on an area of expertise. Endorsements are a quick and kind gesture that I recommend doing frequently. In addition to the good karma, you also reappear on that person's profile. The person then receives an alert that you endorsed, which can serve as a reminder to reconnect. When you receive an endorsement, leave the person a note to say thank you. You may even want to offer the person a cup of coffee or lunch.

If you followed the previous steps to grow your network on LinkedIn, you should now be receiving acceptance notifications to your connection requests. As you receive these notifications, consider endorsing your new contact. What a perfect way to say thank you for connecting.

Adding Recommendations

The next step in building a stellar LinkedIn profile is to add recommendations. Many people have difficulty asking for recommendations. The best way to do this is to begin by asking the people closest to you who you have worked with.

Under the Profile tab, select Recommendations to get started. Follow these steps:

1. Choose what you want to be recommended for. Select the position or school you're asking for a recommendation for.
2. Decide who you will ask. You can ask many people here, but I would avoid it. Recommendations are an important part of your LinkedIn profile, so ask person one at a time.

3. Create a personal message when asking for a recommendation. Don't use the generic message that LinkedIn automatically provides. Instead, write a personal request. Remind the person how you worked together and why you're seeking his recommendation. Depending on your relationship, you may be able to provide further details about key points you want him to highlight.

A LinkedIn recommendation is a modern-day version of the traditional letter of recommendation from a previous employer. Unlike the traditional letter, it can be made public for anyone visiting your profile. Recommendations are like badges of honor and establish confidence in your professional performance for anyone visiting your profile.

Writing Recommendations

Earlier this year, I had a person request a recommendation from me who I had met at a conference. We had never worked together professionally, nor had we done business together. I like the person very much, but I was thrown off when she requested a recommendation. I felt badly, but I had to kindly decline her request.

Your recommendation is your word. If you have no professional history with someone requesting a recommendation, you need to nicely express why you can't provide one. You need to keep the same idea in mind when requesting your own recommendations. Make sure you have had a professional or academic relationship with the person you ask for a recommendation from. This isn't like recommending a restaurant that you hear good things about but have never eaten at. This is closer to recommending a luxury automobile to a close friend. Think of the investment someone who trusts you may make based on your referral.

What if a LinkedIn connection who trusts your word decides to hire someone based on your recommendation? If you have no actual business experience with the person you recommend, it could go horribly wrong. Just consider the cost of hiring and training someone only to end up firing and having to rehire and retrain that position later. Will people still value your word?

Be sure to consider writing recommendations carefully. Next to introductions, a recommendation is probably the most important thing you can do on LinkedIn. You probably will read the reviews of a movie before venturing out to a theater to see it. The same applies to how human resources refer to a candidate's recommendations. Be honest when writing a recommendation, and be appreciative when you receive one.

Sharing Great Content

Like all great social networks, sharing good content goes a long way. Use LinkedIn daily to share a few articles you find online that you think will be beneficial to your network. Add a question or commentary to stir debate or discussions.

Use LinkedIn to promote your blog content, too. There's no harm in promoting your own content, but do so with moderation. Always aim to promote other people's content more frequently than your own. Only share your content that you feel will benefit your LinkedIn network.

Joining Groups

LinkedIn has more than one million groups[6] dedicated to just about every professional topic. Determine which groups are most appropriate for you to join based on your professional goals. You can also visit the profiles of your colleagues to see which groups they belong to. If you work in the same industry, you may choose to join.

Benefits of joining groups include networking with fellow professionals in your industry; meeting potential employees, employers, or clients; and being able to contact group members directly without needing to know their email addresses.

Request to join the groups that interest you most. You can also look through the content to help you decide whether you want to join. Look for warning signs that the group may not be appropriate for you. For example, it may not have an active community. You can see this by checking the dates of the most recent posts. You may also see a large amount of spam in the messages. This is a sign that the group may not be well moderated. Take note of when the most recent updates were posted, and review them to see what they were.

 Tip

In any group, choose Statistics under the More tab. You will discover key information to help determine whether the group is for you. Stats include number of members, location, professional functions, seniority of its members, growth, and level of activity.

When you sign up for a group, decide how frequently you want email summaries sent. LinkedIn can mail you daily or weekly digests with the latest happenings in the group. These emails can quickly clog up your inbox, so decide on a pace that works best for you.

Christopher S. Penn and John Wall manage their LinkedIn group for their popular marketing podcast, "Marketing Over Coffee." They have strict rules, which they remind their listeners of frequently. They encourage their members to flag spam. Chris and John humorously remind members often that if they break the rules, they will be publicly shamed.

I have been guilty of joining LinkedIn groups and not participating frequently enough. By joining too many groups, you will become overwhelmed with the number of messages you receive. Choose just a handful of groups that appeal to you most. Join in the conversations and help people. Don't overly promote yourself or your company, or you'll be asked to leave—or worse, shamed. Take note that you are limited to joining only 50 groups.

Participating in a LinkedIn group can quickly make you a recognized expert in a certain topic. By sharing your knowledge and interacting with the members, you meet new people and ultimately grow your network. Visit New-Networking.com to join our LinkedIn group to share your success stories and tips.

Creating a LinkedIn Group

Once you've familiarized yourself with LinkedIn groups and become a frequent member of a few, you may decide it's time to create your own. Groups are a fantastic way for you to build and lead a community and to market yourself. If you are passionate about a topic, you will gain recognition among your group members as a leader and connector. An added bonus is that you can send messages to your group members, even if they are not connected with you.

There are two options when creating a group: open (public) and closed (private). A closed group is a good way to provide exclusive content and resources to a special selection of people, like your coworkers or customers. An open group has many more benefits, though, that you should consider.

Open groups' content is indexed by search engines, which means you may gain new members from someone searching on Google. Your content can be easily shared across LinkedIn, Facebook, Google+, and Twitter, which will get more eyeballs to your group. Open groups grow much more quickly because of how easily the content can be shared and because...it's an "open" group.

Once your group is set up and ready, it's time to add members. Within your group is an option to Share Group. Share your group by announcing it on your profile using the Share on LinkedIn option. You should also choose to Invite Others by selecting who among your connections you think would like to be a member.

Promote your LinkedIn group across your social profiles, too. Include a link on your splash page. Write a blog post about it, and invite your readers to participate.

You may also want to add a link to your group in your email signature. Remember that quality over quantity is key; you want to have a positive group of smart participating people rather than a group with thousands of members who never visit.

Setting Rules

Set your rules so your members understand and have been warned. It's important to tell members upfront that they need to refrain from being self-promotional. You also don't want members soliciting their products and services. Nobody likes spam.

Rules for your group should be written in a positive, fun way. Don't scare off potential members. Include certain points in your rules, like prohibiting self-promotion and unsolicited spam offers. You may want to remind members to use professional language. You can choose to ask members to refrain from writing negative posts about companies or people. I recommend adding some lighter language at the end of your rules that welcomes them or asks them to enjoy the group.

MARKETING OVER COFFEE'S LINKEDIN GROUP HAS ONE OF MY FAVORITE SETS OF RULES[7]

"We're taking a little more interest in our LinkedIn group here, since just about every other marketing group on LI has turned into a giant can of spam, which is not delicious. In order to keep this little island of LinkedIn free of the junk, we're announcing the following policies:

1. You may be unceremoniously deleted and banned at any time without cause.

2. You may be ceremoniously deleted, banned, and publicly mocked on the show for cause, like trying to fill the group discussion and news with spam, self-promotion, and so forth.

3. Crowdsourced banhammers have been turned on. You can collectively ban posts and flag stuff for attention and removal.

4. There's very little value in just reposting stuff from other sites like Mashable, Techcrunch, etc. We all have Google Reader or an equivalent and are perfectly capable of reading blogs. If there's content you want to share, share it with your commentary, question, etc., so that there's some value added to it besides, "This was cool." Straight reposts of other people's stuff without some explanation of why you think it's important will be visited by a

Death Knight with an axe. We hope these rules strike fear or at least mild discomfort into the self-promoting annoyances that are trolling every other marketing forum.

Enjoy the coffee!"

Once your group is up and running, you can use it to send one announcement per week. This doesn't mean that you *must* send an announcement, but it's an opportunity to check in with the members.

Share interesting links to articles, but add commentary or questions with the link. Ask your members what interesting stories they've read recently. Encourage your members to share the group (assuming it is an open group) publicly with their Facebook, Twitter, and LinkedIn contacts to grow it further.

You should also promote your group across your own social profiles, but be sure to write an original message. Don't stick with the default one that LinkedIn generates. Tell me why you think I should join your group.

You can also send individual invitations with a personal message via LinkedIn. This is a great way for you to grow your group with quality members. As I just wrote, be sure to include a custom invitation to the group.

Most importantly, be active! Don't build the group only to neglect it. Participate and find out how you can help your members. There are opportunities to connect your members to your contacts as well. Remember that to grow your network effectively, you need to find ways to assist others.

Seeing Who's Been Snooping on You

Did you know you can see who has recently viewed your profile? If you're a Pro member, you can see who recently viewed your profile. Basic LinkedIn members also get to see a few of these visitors. Take note who they are.

On the right side of the page is the heading Who's Viewed Your Profile. Click it to reveal some of the people who have visited your profile recently. Who are they? Are they recruiters? Sales people? Former colleagues? Potential clients?

This may give you some insight into who is interested in you. Click through the profiles available to learn more about who they are. This may be a good opportunity to reach out by writing them a message. Remember that you may surprise them, though. Not everyone realizes their views are being tracked. On that note, remember that they can also see you snooping.

Thank you for visiting my profile recently. Please let me know if you have any questions or if I can be of service. I am happy to help you however I can.

Have a great day,

Dave

Basic Profile Analytics

Under the section that reveals who has been looking at your profile, you will notice the number of times you have shown up in search results recently. This is a good figure to take note of and aim to increase, because the more people who are looking at your profile, the more interest you're gaining. An increase in this number indicates that you're improving your use of LinkedIn.

When you're reviewing who has looked at your profile, you will see a small graph on the right side of the page titled Trends. The Trends chart shows you the number of views your profile has received. You can also select the number of times your profile has appeared in search results by month.

By being active in groups by asking and answering questions, you will see visits to your profile increase. Be sure to promote your LinkedIn profile across your social channels, in your email signature, and anywhere else that you think people may click through for a visit. The more visitors to your profile, the more possible job and sales leads may come.

Additional Information

Paying for a LinkedIn Premium account reveals additional information:

- **Top search keywords**—This gives you more insight as to how people are finding you.
- **Viewers by industry**—Perhaps there is an industry taking notice of you that you were not aware of.
- **Viewers by geography**—Are you looking for employment or possible employees from a specific market? Do you focus your business in a general area? This may reveal potential business opportunities elsewhere.
- **Who's checking you out**—You can view everyone who has viewed your profile.

Advanced Search

LinkedIn has a comprehensive Advanced Search (Figure 4.1) feature that allows you to find exactly who you are seeking, whether it is for potential employees, employers, clients, or business promotional partners. Visit linkedin.com/search?trk=advsrch to get started.

Let's say you're searching for human resource managers in Denver. I entered *HR Manager* under Title and 80219 under Zip Code. This resulted in 9,283 profiles.

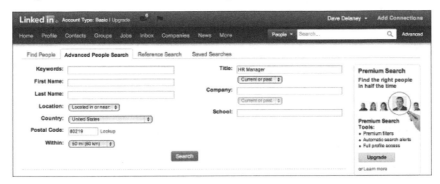

Figure 4.1 *LinkedIn Advanced Search.*

You can segment the results to those who are members of a group you belong to. This is a fantastic way to really narrow the results to a specific target of people you want to connect with.

If you're a member of a group, you use advanced search to search the group's members to see who you have a first-degree connection with. It's a good way to find out if your LinkedIn contacts have joined the group.

There are additional advanced search queries you can perform with a LinkedIn Premium account, such as seniority level and Fortune 1,000. These additional types of searches can help you drill down to find exactly the type of people you're looking for.

I call Advanced Search a secret weapon, because it can enable you to find the important people you need to connect with to advance your career or improve your business. Use it to find potential new employees, employers, sales leads, or industry peers you simply want to network with.

Looking for Work?

If you're on the hunt for employment, visit linkedin.com/jobs. Using the Advanced Search function, you can find industry-specific positions narrowed down by zip or postal code.

Assuming you have followed my directions in this chapter to make plenty of great connections on LinkedIn and to grow your network, you will see who you know at each company with open positions.

According to a study by Jobvite titled "Social Recruiting Survey 2012,"[8] which included a poll of more than 1,000 HR professionals and recruiters, 93% were using LinkedIn to find candidates.

The study found that the use of LinkedIn for the purpose of finding qualified candidates has grown substantially from 87% in 2011 and 78% in 2010. It's essential that a job seeker has her LinkedIn profile up to date and optimized for potential recruitment efforts.

Be sure to follow the pages of the company you want to work for. You can learn plenty by doing so, plus they may take notice of you as a new follower. To do so, click the Follow button on the right side of any company page.

Creating Partnerships for Your Company

Many people incorrectly think that LinkedIn is strictly used for employment. While career advancement is certainly a key goal of using LinkedIn, it can also be used to create partnerships for a business. One of the best business uses I have found for LinkedIn is to get introductions to potential promotional partners. As a marketing professional, I'm always thinking of ways to use promotions to benefit the companies involved and ultimately, the consumers.

I worked with Griffin Technology at the time the iPhone 3G was released. Because the iPhone camera couldn't shoot macro photos clearly, Griffin designed the Clarifi case, which included a sliding close-up lens to rectify the problem.

At that time, Evernote was emerging as a leader in iPhone applications. The clever company created an app that would help the user remember things. You could use it to record audio notes to yourself, write notes, or take photos.

What makes Evernote amazing is its ability to use optical character recognition (OCR). This means that you can snap a photo of text—let's say a receipt, for example. Once it's uploaded, you can use the search engine to search text within the image. The trouble Evernote users were experiencing was not because of their app, but that the iPhone camera lens could not keep focused at close ranges and therefore produced blurry up-close photos.

I saw an immediate opportunity to align Griffin with Evernote so we could create a giveaway of Clarifi cases to Evernote users (see Figure 4.2). This would help promote the case to a new group of potential customers while Griffin would promote Evernote to their customers.

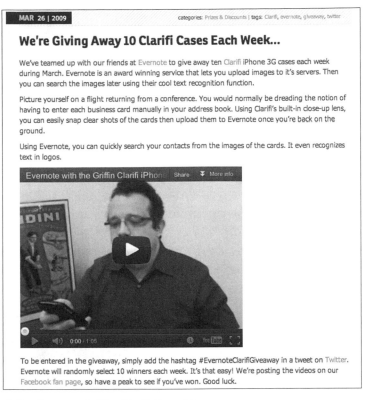

Figure 4.2 *Evernote Griffin Clarifi Case Giveaway.*

The one problem was that I didn't know anyone at Evernote. Cold-calling seemed inappropriate, and general mailbox email addresses often go unanswered. Besides, I was excited for the opportunity to work with them quickly.

I turned to my LinkedIn connections. By having a large, robust group of contacts in my network, I was able to search and find a person who was connected to someone at Evernote. My contact was a friend, so I simply had to email her to ask for an introduction. Before I knew it, I was talking to Evernote, and our cobranded giveaway was launched to great success for all parties.

This is the power of LinkedIn. As I mentioned, the important point is to build the network before you need it.

LinkedIn Company Pages

Up until now, I have been writing with the full purpose of you growing your personal/professional network using LinkedIn. This is a must, first and foremost. The next stop is your business page, whether it's your own personal business or the company you work for.

A January 2012 study from HubSpot[9] found that LinkedIn generated the highest visitor-to-lead conversion rate at 2.74%, almost three times higher (277%) than both Twitter (.69%) and Facebook (.77%). This is a telling metric of why you should consider a LinkedIn company page. It clearly is the winner in driving qualified traffic to your site.

Remember that you will be using LinkedIn primarily for networking. That is what this book is about, after all. However, it's wise to provide your company details on its own page. If somebody wants to learn more about you, she will likely want to learn about your business, too. Interested future employees, customers, and investors also may follow your company on LinkedIn. Take note of who is following you and learn more about them by clicking the Follower Insights button on your page.

Visit linkedin.com/company/add/show to begin the process. It's relatively easy to follow the steps to create your page. One amazing example is Dell's company page. Use LinkedIn's search window, choose Companies, and search for *Dell*. Dell has great graphics and up-to-date information and is actively participating as you see in Figure 4.3.

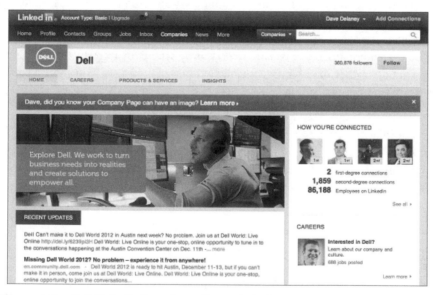

Figure 4.3   *Dell LinkedIn Page: https://www.linkedin.com/company/1093.*

Use the Products and Services section to share what your company can offer. Use the same SEO techniques I outlined in Chapter 3 to be sure you're using optimized keywords and terms to describe your business. You can also post videos and links to your site here.

Use the Company Status updates section to share links to company news and relevant industry-related information. As you share links, be sure to return to your page frequently to reply to any comments left. Remember that the purpose is to build relationships with your customers.

Check the Insights section to see other companies that visitors to your page also viewed. This may reveal potential competitors. The Insights section also provides analytics like page views, page visitor demographics, unique visitors, and more.

Like most social networking sites, LinkedIn company pages provide a Follow button that you can add on your splash page, blog, email signature, or elsewhere.

Generating Leads for Your Company

A friend of mine worked for a company whose sales manager scolded his team for spending time on LinkedIn. He was worried they were using the social network to update their resumes and find new jobs when they were actually networking to find new sales leads.

By using LinkedIn, you can research an industry and find people you should connect with for business development. For example, a catering company may choose to connect to hotels or event planners in their region, or a photographer may contact wedding planners. Be sure to do this by asking for introductions with your connections rather than sending unsolicited InMail messages. You should be networking and not spamming.

Consider creating a free eBook or whitepaper sharing insight about your profession or industry. Brand it with your company logo and information. Use your LinkedIn page and profile to promote the download. You can also create polls on your LinkedIn company page and encourage people to vote on the topics. This will drive traffic to your page, generate potential new leads, and help to grow your network.

I also recommend asking your current clients for referrals. Recommendations are just as important on your LinkedIn company page as they are on your personal LinkedIn profile. Jay Moonah is vice president of marketing at Wild Apricot, a software company that provides membership software for associations, nonprofits, clubs, and subscription websites. Jay explained that Wild Apricot (see Figure 4.4) has seen an increase of 15% in conversions on its site from using LinkedIn's recommendations. It actively requests recommendations from its customers.

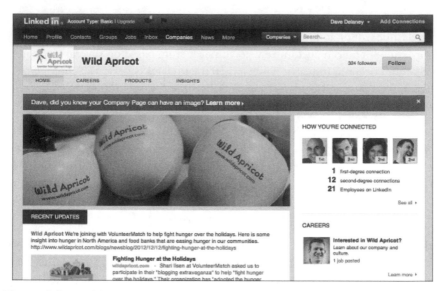

Figure 4.4   *Wild Apricot LinkedIn Page https://www.linkedin.com/company/1194245.*

Backing Up

One feature of LinkedIn that members are often not aware of is the Export Contacts function. I'm a firm believer that you should always back up your important data, because if your account gets hacked or you lose access, you may not be able to retrieve your data. Why risk losing the ability to reach your network that you took so long to nurture and build?

I expect you now agree with the importance of a strong LinkedIn network, so take the time to back up your connections. You can do this by selecting the Contacts tab and choosing Export below the directory near the bottom of the page.

Back up this file both locally on your computer and by attaching it to an email to yourself. This is important personal information and should be treated that way.

I print out my list of contacts from time to time to review it. I consider who I can help in my network by providing an introduction to someone else. Remember that networking is not only about what your network can do for you, but about what you can do for your network.

LinkedIn Signal

Like every social network, LinkedIn can become overwhelming as you grow your network. One lesser-known section is called LinkedIn Signal. Signal makes

a perfect home page to your LinkedIn experience. It creates a fully customizable dashboard for a quick overview of trending stories and updates from your connections. You can customize who you hear from based on several settings, including Location, Industry, Time (when the updates occurred), School, Group, Topics, Seniority, and Update Type (such as Connection, Profiles, Shares, Groups, Company, News). It is a powerful tool for searching within the site.

Visit www.linkedin.com/signal. On the left side of the page under "Network," you can see a list of your personal updates on LinkedIn by clicking "By Me." This includes endorsements you have received and posts you have made. If you select "1st Connections," the page will be refreshed with the most recent updates from your closest connections. There is also the option of selecting "2nd Connections" or "3rd Connections" to broaden your search results.

Select "Company" and take a peek at the most recent updates from a company's staff and page. LinkedIn Signal will show each company you have a connection with, plus it has a search option to search for any company with a LinkedIn page. You can see who has connected with whom, who has recently been endorsed, and company news.

The best part of Signal is that you can combine each search. For example, you can search for 2nd Connections who work for Google, are based in Ireland, and attended University College Dublin. Signal's search is an indispensable tool to help you find and focus on specific people and companies.

LinkedIn Connection Update

As you grow your network of contacts in LinkedIn, you will begin to receive email updates when a person has changed positions. This can vary from a person moving to a different company to someone changing titles within the same firm.

One challenge as you grow your network is to keep up appearances. It's impossible to be everywhere all the time. The connection update emails you receive give you a reason to reach out to congratulate a person on her new role and to reconnect.

The connection update emails can be a little overwhelming. If you prefer, you can use a third-party service like jobchangenotifier.com to follow updates online on selected people and companies. This is a good alternative option, because you can track specific individuals.

Be sure to download LinkedIn's mobile app for the most popular devices from linkedin.com/mobile. This is a must for any professional person seeking new connections, great content, and updates from peers. I check the app as part of my morning routine to see and share news stories that I believe my connections will

find useful. You can also get connection updates, answer questions, and scan for new discussion topics in groups you belong to. You can even start your own discussions.

CardMunch is another must-get LinkedIn app for busy networkers. There are plenty of good business card scanning apps, but CardMunch connects directly into your LinkedIn contacts. You can snap a photo of the business cards of the people that you meet at an event or conference and upload the information directly into LinkedIn—all from the comfort of your iPhone. An Android version is coming soon, too.

TripIt is an application that can automatically share where you travel to and from. It's an ideal way to automatically inform your LinkedIn contacts of where you will be next. This is good to track to see who is coming to your city. Perhaps a catch-up lunch is due to be scheduled.

Grow Your Network Before You Need It

If you choose any social network to grow your career and build your business, it should be LinkedIn. I will share my advice on building your professional networks on other social networks in the next chapters. However, LinkedIn is by far the leading professional social network. Use it to grow your network now, before you need it. You will be thankful later.

Remember the importance of helping to connect others. Use LinkedIn to endorse and write recommendations for the people you want to promote. Join appropriate groups to interact and meet fellow professionals to share useful content, elaborate on topics, and answer questions.

I warned you in Chapter 1, "Do Your Homework," that I would repeatedly remind you that networking is a two-way street. Consider this your Chapter 4 reminder.

Endnotes

1. www.forbes.com/sites/jacquelynsmith/2012/04/03/what-employers-need-to-know-about-the-class-of-2012/

2. www.bls.gov/news.release/empsit.nr0.htm

3. http://press.linkedin.com/about

4. http://press.linkedin.com/about

5. http://mashable.com/2012/05/27/resume-tracking-systems/

6. http://mashable.com/2011/11/03/linkedin-numbers-q3-2011/

7. https://www.linkedin.com/groups?gid=1768847&trk=myg_ugrp_ovr

8. http://news.cnet.com/8301-1023_3-57469282-93/heads-up-linkedin-users-93-of-recruiters-are-looking-at-you/

9. http://blog.hubspot.com/blog/tabid/6307/bid/30030/LinkedIn-277-More-Effective-for-Lead-Generation-Than-Facebook-Twitter-New-Data.aspx#ixzz2DifgSeHE

5

Building a Network, 140 Characters at a Time: Twitter

When I speak about Twitter at conferences and seminars, I always ask the room how many people have an account. I follow this up by asking how many people tweet every day. The difference is usually about half. Twitter is mentioned daily, whether via a sporting event, a popular television show, a commercial, the news, or the Web. Ninety percent of Americans are aware of Twitter.[1]

We're asked to follow Twitter accounts constantly, but seldom are we told why we should be following. What's in it for me? So many people still don't fully understand how or why they should be using Twitter. But when Twitter is used well, it can be a powerful place to grow your network.

Background

I sent my first tweet in February 2007, and I became quite active at that time. I found connecting with complete strangers and talking about topics I was interested in to be exciting. It reminded me of my early days communicating online via IRC (Internet Relay Chat) chat rooms. Have I just dated myself?

Even very early on, I saw the value in networking using Twitter. During a presentation about Twitter in 2008 at BarCamp Nashville, I asked the small room of attendees to use Twitter to share a link to help raise money for a needy classroom in Middle Tennessee. I watched with excitement as the attendees picked up their phones or began tapping away on their laptops. By the end of my 20-minute presentation, we raised $500 from the audience and their personal networks on Twitter. It was not my intention to do this to increase followers, but I did see a spike in new followers during this campaign.

Plenty of things have changed with Twitter over the years: its design, the company's relationship with developers, the services, its stability, the introduction of lists, and more. When you get right down to it, though, Twitter is fundamentally still the same free microblogging service.

The Basics

When you create an account on Twitter and send your first tweet, the immediate results may be lackluster. People need to be following you to see what you have to say. Don't give up. With some tender loving care, patience, and perseverance, you will have a small following in no time. All Twitter accounts start with zero followers.

Creating your account on Twitter takes little time. As you do it, you will be walked through a few demo screens to familiarize you with how it works. You will see an example of the timeline and a tweet. You will be asked to follow five accounts. Twitter provides some suggested users such as pop stars, news anchors, authors, and technology leaders. You can also search for a topic you're interested in and follow accounts from the results. I welcome you to search for @davedelaney and follow me. Please be sure to say hello when you do.

The next screen provides you with categories of interest. You're asked to follow five accounts from any of the categories. They range from music to books, and sports to humor. Don't let the default categories fool you. Just about every topic you can think of is likely being tweeted about by any of Twitter's approximately 500 million users.[2]

The step that follows is the most important one. Twitter searches your email accounts to find your contacts who are on Twitter. Follow the profiles of your friends, family, customers, colleagues, and everyone you know who is on Twitter. This is how it all begins.

Don't know many people on Twitter? I will write more about how to find potential employees, employers, customers, and interesting and fun people to follow in this chapter using lists and third-party services.

Types of Tweets

Great tweets should fit into one of four categories: inspirational, informative, advocating, or entertaining.

Inspirational

Share an inspirational quote, or better yet, write your own. Write something that inspires thought and inspires action, like you see in Figures 5.1 and 5.2.

Figure 5.1   *@johnmorgan.*

Figure 5.2   *@zen_habits.*

Informative

Share interesting news, factoids, and tips that your followers will find interesting, as shown in Figures 5.3 and 5.4.

Figure 5.3   *@jolieodell.*

Figure 5.4   *@dmscott.*

Advocating

Use Twitter to promote other people before promoting yourself or your own content. In Figure 5.5, Chris Brogan helps to spread the word about artist Christian Soucy, who needs some help getting through the holidays. In Figure 5.6, C.C. Chapman spreads the word about Charity Water, who is building wells for people in Ethiopia.

Figure 5.5   *@chrisbrogan.*

Figure 5.6   *@cc_chapman.*

Entertaining

Who doesn't love a good song or laugh? Share the good stuff. I retweeted both of the tweets you see in Figures 5.7 and 5.8 for a laugh.

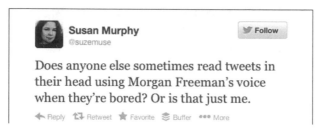

Figure 5.7   *@suzemuse*

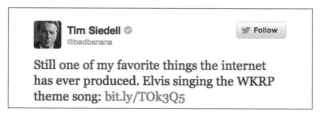

Figure 5.8   *@badbanana.*

I've always respected author and social media marketing expert Chris Brogan's 12:1 ratio.[3] Chris believes that we should reserve a self-promotional tweet for once every twelve tweets that we promote someone else. I couldn't agree more.

Chris Brogan is an amazing example of a person who regularly delivers tweets that fit into one of the four categories. You should follow him @chrisbrogan.

Brevity and Direct Messages

Twitter users send short messages totaling 140 characters. Brevity is key. The 140 character count is due to the limit of 160 characters in regular text messages. Twitter chose 140 characters to keep 20 characters reserved for the recipient's username. Consider having a short username if possible. My friend Rex Hammock is lucky enough to be @r on Twitter!

The messages or "tweets" you compose can include links to interesting news or blog content, videos, and photos. People use Twitter to interact with one another by using the @ symbol before the user's name. The tweet then appears in that user's timeline and on your own. If you were sending a tweet to me, you would include @davedelaney.

Most users will follow you in return for following them, but there's no written rule about who you should follow and whether they must follow you back. Once a user is following you back, you can send that person a private message called a DM, or direct message. You certainly want to grow your follower base. The more people who follow you, the further your tweets will spread. However, you shouldn't obsess about your number of followers. Instead, focus on sharing great content and replying and promoting other people frequently by sharing their content and retweeting their best tweets. You will soon see your followers increase, because people will take notice of the quality of your tweets.

Retweets

A retweet is an easy way to share something you enjoy on Twitter written by someone else. When you see a tweet you like, you press the Retweet button. Avoid going nuts retweeting everyone's tweets. Be selective, but do share some of the good content you happen upon. Not only will your followers notice the good content you're sharing, but the creators of the original tweets will too, if they are tracking their retweets. If you want to be sure the original source of the tweet sees your retweet, skip the retweet button and compose the tweet using the letters "RT" instead, which the original composer will see as a reply. The advantage of using RT instead of Twitter's retweet button is you can add your own commentary to the tweet.

When I see someone retweet one of my tweets, I take notice of who they are. I may take a moment to thank them for the retweet, and I will likely follow them. Retweets can result in meeting new people and growing your network on Twitter.

Hat Tips

Be sure to always credit a source of an article or original tweet. You can do this by using the Retweet button, but another way is to include HT @username. The HT stands for hat tip, symbolizing a tip of the hat to the original source. This is good Twitter etiquette.

Let's say you see a tweet from me about an interesting story. If you include HT @davedelaney in the tweet, I will notice it, because you used my name.

Goals

If you plan to spend time on Twitter or any social networking site, you need to set some goals and review your performance regularly. Twitter goals can include increasing your follower growth, gaining traffic from Twitter to your personal blog or company site, and increasing your retweets. What is it you hope to accomplish?

Obviously, networking is my goal when using Twitter. I absolutely love to meet new people and keep connected with friends. By sharing valuable links to articles related to social media marketing, my followers know what to expect since the topic is a passion of mine. However, I also use Twitter to share the human side of me, the one that is easily amused by quick, witty anecdotes and obscure photos. I love seeing a retweet or a reply with an LOL. It shows that people find my content valuable or amusing.

Take a moment to think about what you're trying to achieve most on Twitter. What are your goals? Use a spreadsheet to enter the metrics that matter most to you, and fill it in weekly to track your performance. I'll discuss tools that you can track metrics such as follower growth, retweets, and more in this chapter. A key goal should be to enjoy Twitter. You should be having fun interacting, retweeting, and connecting with people.

Finding Interesting People

Aside from importing your contacts from your email address book and database, you can use services like Followerwonk.com to search bios and city names. It's a fantastic tool to search for people with specific job titles within a geographic location. For example, you can search for "CEO" in Kansas City, Missouri, or "Engineer" in New Orleans, Louisiana.

If you're following a popular person in your industry who has many followers, you may choose to use a service like Tweepi.com to follow that person's followers. If you find that you've followed someone you're no longer interested in following, you can unfollow him later. You can also use Tweepi to follow members of a public Twitter list. I'll write more on Twitter lists shortly.

I mentioned Rapportive in Chapter 1, "Do Your Homework." Use it within your email to find the Twitter profile of the person you're writing to. If this is a sales lead or human resources manager, you can review that person's profile without following the person to learn more about him.

Calvin Lee @mayhemstudios

Calvin Lee @mayhemstudios is a superstar on Twitter (see Figure 5.9). He also frequently attends technology conferences and festivals. Calvin is an award-winning designer and brand strategist at Mayhem Studios. He's also a popular person on Twitter, with nearly 80,000 followers. Using Twitter, he has connected with influencers, and many professional relationships have come from his efforts.

Figure 5.9 *@mayhemstudios.*

Guy Kawasaki, Apple's first evangelist and well-known public speaker and author, was a person Calvin wanted to connect to. Calvin decided to regularly tweet to Guy, mention him, and retweet Guy's tweets, hoping to get a response.

Guy took notice and began to banter back and forth with Calvin on Twitter. One day, Guy asked Calvin if he would be attending an upcoming conference. Calvin had never attended a technology conference before, but he did with the expectation of meeting Guy in person. It worked!

Calvin and Guy enjoyed lunch together, and Guy asked Calvin to design some business cards. Besides designing the business cards, Calvin was hired to help design banners on Guy's popular website AllTop.com.

Networking on Twitter can result in professional opportunities for you, but it's important to focus on the people you truly want to connect with. Calvin was inspired by Guy's work, so it was a natural fit for him to try to get to know Guy better using Twitter.

Be Careful, Be Healthy

It has always been good Twitter etiquette to follow people back who follow you. Unfortunately, many spam bot accounts have been created that automatically follow you. In some cases, these can be malicious accounts made to tempt you to click a link, which can result in malware being installed on your computer. Review the profiles of your followers, and follow the ones you find interesting. If you receive a DM from a follower with a strange link, think before you click it. The link may lead to malware or other malicious content.

To use the many free applications that improve Twitter, you need to sign in with your Twitter account. You should never have to enter your password. Signing up

for services is fine, but always be wary and check to see if others recommended them. You will probably find reference to services on Mashable.com, a popular social media news and resources site.

From time to time, it's wise to visit the Settings section of your Twitter profile and revoke permissions to the apps you're no longer using. Out with the old, in with the new!

To maintain a healthy Twitter account, keep your follower/following ratio in check. Avoid following more people than the number of people following you. Accounts that are following hundreds or thousands of people with few followers could be a sign that something is suspicious. Twitter may feel that way, too. Remember to focus on quality over quantity. Strive to follow smart people who complement your network, not everyone and her brother or sister. The best networking comes from following and interacting with great people.

Twitter Is a Cocktail Party

I think of Twitter like a cocktail party. I'm not the first person to use this analogy, but it's the one I find to be most accurate. There are standard best practices to Twitter that are similar to those you would follow at a cocktail party.

Keep Self-Promotion to a Minimum

Nobody likes the excessive talker at a cocktail party. You know the guy. He won't stop talking about who he is and what he does. It's fine to tell someone what you do, but inquire about what she does first. Most of the time the person you ask will explain, and then follow up by asking you the same question. You will grow your network (followers) much more effectively by not trying to sell people something. Instead, list and follow the people you find most interesting; they will probably reciprocate and follow you, too.

Introduce People You Admire to One Another

When I learn about a specialty that a person does, I try to introduce that person to someone who has a similar interest. Sometimes I may even introduce that person to a news reporter or author who is looking for an expert. One great way to grow your network is to help people grow their own. Not only will they be grateful to you for making the connection, but they may tell others about how helpful you were, which will result in gaining even more followers.

Make Quality Small Talk

Twitter is all about small talk—140 characters at a time. Ask questions and reply to the answers. Also reply to other people's questions and comments. Think about what you're sharing. Is it helpful? Share interesting articles, stories, jokes, and what's on your mind. Add a question about the story to kick-start the conversation. By providing good conversation starters, you grow your network from the interactions, and new follows occur as a result. At first, Twitter can seem underwhelming, because you feel like you are tweeting to an empty room. As you find and gain followers, your tweets will be seen by more people. Make quality small talk, and you will grow your Twitter community over time.

Find the People You Have Things in Common With

It's estimated that Twitter has 500 million registered users.[4] Surely, someone has similar interests to yours, right? By using steps that I'll explain in a moment, you will find interesting people to follow and ultimately grow your network. Connecting with people in your industry or with similar interests benefits everyone involved, because you can share knowledge, provide insight, and make introductions to other people who share your passion.

Listen Carefully

Smart people listen well on Twitter. Listen to what people are telling you. Use Twitter search and third-party tools to listen carefully to the conversations taking place. By listening, you become wiser. Be proactive by creating custom searches for keywords, terms related to your line of work, your name (and misspellings of it), and topics you're interested in. I'll explain this further later in this chapter.

Follow Up

Follow the people you find interesting on Twitter. You can create a list to follow specific people using Twitter lists. Be sure to stay on the radar of the people you want to further speak with. Relationships won't grow if you just push out a tweet and reply. By keeping up appearances and interacting frequently, you'll strengthen these relationships. Keep the conversation going, and pay attention to the people you want to build a relationship with. Your network will become bigger and better the more quality people you include. Share the tweets from the people you most enjoy. It's an easy way to promote others.

Creating and Following Lists

Back in 2007, there was no option to create lists of Twitter accounts. People used a public wiki page to add themselves under different topic headings hoping that others would refer to it to find and follow them. This all changed in October 2009 when Twitter officially launched Lists.

Twitter Lists give you the option to group people you're interested in into a public list or a private list, so all list member's tweets appear in one feed. A public list can be shared so other people may decide to follow it. For example, the *New York Times* has a public list called NYT Journalists that includes 515 of its reporters, editors, photographers, and producers. (See http://twitter.com/nytimes/nyt-journalists.)

A private list can help you keep track of those closest to you, like friends or family. Consider creating a private list to follow your best customers and industry influencers, so you can be quick to interact with them frequently. You don't have to follow individual Twitter accounts to add them to a private list. This means that the Twitter user won't know he's been added, which is useful for a business that wants to follow its competitors on Twitter.

To network effectively, aim to connect with people you have something in common with. Using Twitter lists, you can easily find people with similar interests. When you create or subscribe to a list of people with common interests, you can refer to it frequently, to share and interact. It's the people you share commonalities with who will most likely follow you and build a rapport with you.

It's wise to review the lists that people have included you on from time to time. What are the list topics? You'll likely see similarities between them. For example, many of the lists I'm on refer to social media professionals. Use this information to consider how your network considers you. If you find yourself listed on many lists related to website development, be sure you're providing tweets related to this.

To find out what lists you're on, go to your profile on Twitter and click Lists. This defaults to show the results of the lists you're subscribed to. Next to this is a link called Member Of. You can find this easily by replacing the XXXs with your Twitter profile name: https://twitter.com/XXX/lists/memberships.

If you're not included in any lists, don't worry. Perhaps you're new to Twitter, or you're not tweeting consistently. Tweet about topics that are interesting to you but that are also related to your industry. If you become more consistent with the topics you tweet about, you'll find yourself added to lists before you know it. It's easy to lose hours of productivity while exploring Twitter. By using Twitter lists, your time spent on Twitter will be more efficient and effective. As I mentioned, be sure to follow the people you're interested in on the lists. This will alert them that you've taken an interest. Hopefully they will reciprocate and follow you in return.

Take some time now to consider how you want to be perceived on Twitter. Review the lists you're already on, find lists to follow that align well with your interests, and create a private list of influencers you want to interact with regularly. By using Twitter lists to follow and interact with people with similar interests, you will ultimately grow your network. Not only will you gain *more* followers, but you'll gain *valuable* followers who can help you with your networking efforts and vice versa.

Advanced Search

One of the most valuable ways for a person to use Twitter is to listen to what people are saying (or watch what the people are tweeting, as the case may be). The best way to listen is by using the Advanced Search function (Figure 5.10).

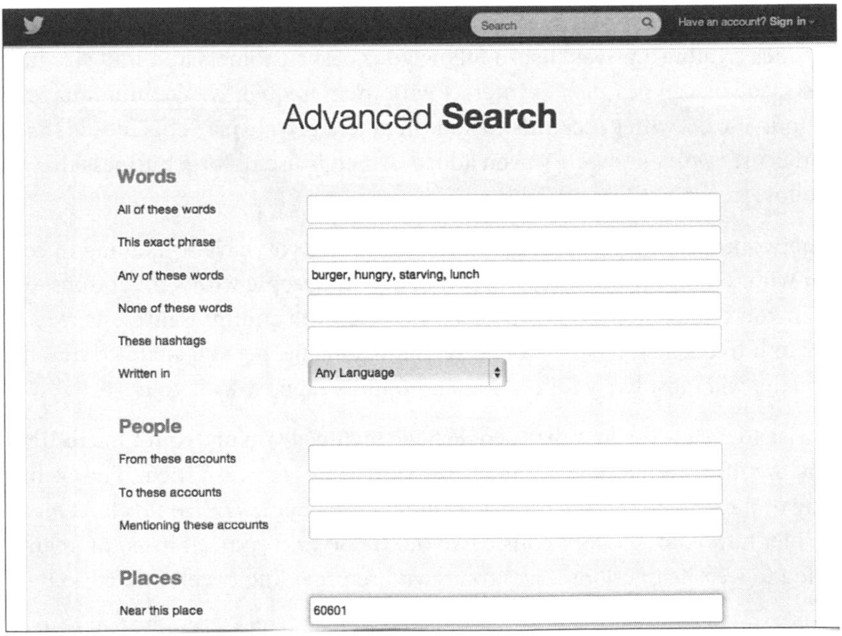

Figure 5.10   *Twitter Advanced Search: https://twitter.com/search-advanced.*

Let's say you own a restaurant in Chicago that specializes in hamburgers. There are probably hundreds of competing restaurants just like yours. Yes, your burger uses organic ingredients. Yes, your restaurant has an eclectic design that makes dining with you a fun experience. Yes, your staff is the best. But not everybody knows about you—yet.

A particularly quiet lunch hour could go down two different ways:

1. You could stand around hoping that you get a sudden rush of customers.

2. You could use your smart phone to find customers using Twitter's Advanced Search.

If you chose 1, best of luck to you. If you chose 2, read on.

Twitter's Advanced Search page has several fields you can fill out to create a customized search. I'll walk you through how best to do this.

Under the Words section, create a search under Any of These Words for *burger*, *hungry*, *starving*, *lunch*. Scroll down to the Places section, and enter your zip code.

Save the results of this search so you can easily return to it. The option to do this is provided by clicking on the gear icon when using your computer. It may look different depending on the mobile app you're using.

You'll see that not all the results are exactly what you're seeking, but you should see some hungry potential customers in your area. This is the perfect opportunity to reply with an offer they can't refuse. How about a free appetizer, free dessert, or discount on their meal?

Try another search under the Words section. Create a search under Any of These Words for *burger hamburger*. Scroll down to Places and enter your zip code. Scroll down to Other, and select the tick box for Question.

The results of this search should show people asking questions related to burgers or hamburgers near your restaurant. Save the results of this search again.

There are many different configurations that you can use Twitter Advanced Search for. Create several searches for topics related to your industry or business. Save the searches, and return to them frequently.

Is your restaurant a little slow today? Pop out your smart phone and check your search results. I bet there's a hungry person just a few blocks away looking for a place to find a decent burger. Give it a try.

Gary Vaynerchuck @garyvee

In the social media marketing space, Gary Vaynerchuck @garyvee is a household name, as seen in Figure 5.11. Gary is a successful speaker, author, and business person who famously used social media to expand his father's liquor store, Shopper's Discount Liquor, into Wine Library, a $60 million a year business.[5]

Figure 5.11   *@garyvee.*

Gary is the poster boy for someone who understands how to use social media effectively to grow his network of nearly 1 million Twitter followers by providing thoughtful, inspiring, and helpful content.

During his 2010 South by Southwest Interactive keynote presentation, Gary shared one of the key ways he grew Wine Library. He used Summize, which was the service used to search Twitter before Twitter acquired it to launch its own search tool.

Gary explained that he built his list and his community by creating searches for types of wine. He would scan the search results and answer questions that people tweeted. He wouldn't respond trying to sell the person anything. He would simply reply with the answer the person was seeking. He organically attracted new followers from being helpful.

Consider how you can use searches on Twitter to help answer questions related to your industry. Don't only think about this as a professional; consider answering questions related to your field of study if you're a student, too. The knowledge you're gaining at school can easily be shared and used to help potential future employers or customers. Get started by setting up some searches today.

Hashtags and Twitter Chats

Just as using the @ symbol before a username is crucial to communicating effectively on Twitter, hashtags are an important way you can search and track conversations. On August 23, 2007, @ChrisMessina introduced the idea of using a hashtag or pound sign to track conversations.[6]

Today, hashtags are used to power Twitter's trending topics. You can also use hashtags to enter contests, follow breaking news stories, discuss politics and

sports, and track conversations during conferences. You can click a hashtag in any tweet to reveal the most recent uses of it. You can also search for hashtags within Twitter's Advanced Search tool.

An example of a hashtag would be the use of #TED2013, representing discussions around the TED conference in 2013. When you use a hashtag, it instantly becomes a link within the tweet. You can click the hashtag and follow the discussions around the conference. Hashtags are also common during major sporting and television events such as #superbowl or #oscars.

A great example of using a hashtag to track a conversation on Twitter is #blogchat. In March 2009, author and social media strategist Mack Collier created his popular weekly blogger chat. It has been going strong ever since.

Every Sunday night from 8 p.m. to 9 p.m. CST, blogging professionals and hobbyists join the conversation in a flurry of more than 1,000 rapid tweets. Mack hosts the hour and brings expert guest hosts who provide insight and information about a wide range of topics, including the best blog plug-ins and widgets, ways of promoting your blog, writing tips, new tools, and more.

I've always enjoyed participating in #blogchat, because experts learn from the participants, and vice versa. Chatting via Twitter is also a great way to meet new people with similar interests. It's an amazing example of using Twitter to grow your network.

It's often difficult to keep up with the tweets during a Twitter chat. People use different tools to track and manage the flow of tweets. I recommend TweetChat.com.

TweetChat connects directly to Twitter, so you can compose tweets and replies directly through the service. It creates a "room" that only shows tweets with the hashtag you're following, so in this case, all I see are the tweets using #blogchat, as shown in Figure 5.12. It also automatically adds the hashtag in your tweets.

In the User Control section of TweetChat, I suggest you choose to Block Retweets. Otherwise, the most popular tweets may appear repeatedly, which will make keeping up with the other tweets more difficult. If you miss something, it's not the end of the world, though, because Mack provides a transcript after each #blogchat.

You can upset your regular Twitter followers if you suddenly flood them with strange tweets. Your regular followers may not be interested in the topic of your tweet chat. It's good Twitter etiquette to warn your followers ahead of time, so they can be prepared for the onslaught of tweets. This is also a good reason to keep Twitter chats to 60 minutes max.

Figure 5.12 *TweetChat.com.*

After your chat, be sure to reply to each tweet you received if you didn't get a chance to already. You should use this time to follow the interesting people you met during the chat to grow and improve the quality of your network.

Let's pretend for a moment that you're attending a conference and the organizers have selected #TZZ2013 as the hashtag. Be sure to use the hashtag when tweeting before, during, or after about the conference. During the conference, you should save a search for the hashtag so you can refer to the *back channel* (conversations on Twitter from the audience).

I recall attending a conference in which a speaker was not clear about a topic he was presenting on. The back channel was on fire (not literally) with many people asking questions about the topic, and experts in the audience answered the questions that the speaker was not answering. The Twitter conversation was by no means bashing the speaker. Instead, attendees were helping to answer questions and clear confusion about the topic. Without a way to track the conversations using a hashtag, this simply could not have happened.

The hashtag was also used to discuss where fellow attendees would be eating after the conference. By following the hashtag, attendees kept together and got to know each other better, thus growing their networks.

Twitter Tools

Hundreds of services and apps can improve your experience on Twitter in one way or another. Some are even must-haves. This section goes over a few of my personal favorites.

HootSuite

HootSuite (Hootsuite.com) provides an extensive browser-based dashboard. You can use it to send and schedule tweets and status updates for Facebook and LinkedIn. It's a great way to monitor your *mentions* (tweets to you or about you), DMs, search results (like tracking a hashtag, for example), and lists you're following. In the paid version, you can have multiple administrators and access to custom analytical reports, which include metrics like number of clicks on a link, follower growth, and retweets. A dashboard like HootSuite helps your networking efforts, because you can see your replies, DMs, search results, and lists all in one place. When you have everything in front of you, communicating via Twitter is much easier.

Commun.it

Commun.it (http://Commun.it) is another dashboard service, similar to HootSuite. This dashboard can help you keep track of the conversations and people who are most important to you personally and professionally. Commun.it also provides suggestions of accounts you should consider following and ones you may decide to unfollow. Further, it groups people you communicate with most frequently, which is an amazing benefit. You can also pay for a pro service that gives you much more analytical information about how your account is performing similar to HootSuite's.

Buffer

Buffer (Bufferapp.com) is a terrific service to help you schedule tweets. It determines the best times of the day for you to deliver tweets to your followers. You can then plug in several tweets ahead of time to be delivered throughout the day or night. Buffer also ties into Facebook and LinkedIn, so you can schedule updates for those services, too.

Ask around, and you will quickly find the topic of scheduling tweets a hot one. One side of the argument feels that scheduling tweets is perfectly fine, whereas others feel it goes against what Twitter is all about. Like it or not, scheduled tweets are used frequently, especially by online marketers and social media professionals. The

important thing to understand is Twitter should be as real-time as possible. If you choose to schedule tweets, be sure the bulk of your tweets are not scheduled.

 Caution

Automation can take a lot of work off your shoulders, but it can also cause you and your followers headaches. For example, I once scheduled a tweet to announce a contest, which I accidentally delivered too early. Social media should be social. Remember to be present to respond to the replies you receive. It's a given that you can't be on Twitter all the time. But if you schedule a tweet, do your best to respond in a timely manner.

Bit.ly

An early problem with Twitter was its limit of 140 characters per tweet. If the link you were sharing was longer than this, it was cut off and wouldn't function. Several link-shrinking services came and left, but Bit.ly (Bitly.com) remained. Today, Twitter automatically shortens your links using its t.co preface. I still prefer Bit.ly because you can customize the link with a word instead of some random characters. You can also view basic analytics from your Bit.ly links, like number of clicks and where geographically the clicks occurred. These basic analytics can help you determine if your network of followers is finding your content click-worthy. They also give you some idea of where your followers are in the world.

Tweet Grader

HubSpot's Tweet Grader (tweet.grader.com) is a free tool to get a report of your performance on Twitter. Take the results with a grain of salt, but use the information revealed to address the suggestions the tool provides. The higher your score, the more likely your Twitter account is up to snuff. I chose a random Twitter account to test using Tweet Grader, and the grade was a score of 32 out of 100. Recommendations included adding a location and bio to the account. Networking on Twitter is more effective when people can find you and can learn more from your bio. Give Tweet Grader a try, and see how high you score.

Twitter Counter

Interested to see how your account stacks up to two others? You can use Twitter Counter (TwitterCounter.com) to compare multiple profiles or just examine your own. It shows you your follower growth over time. See any spikes or dips in your

graph? Take note of the date, and look at your tweets from that day to help determine what might have caused the increase (or decrease) of followers.

Tweetbot

Tweetbot (tapbots.com) is my go-to Twitter iPhone and iPad app. I like Tweetbot because of its easy customization and simple user interface that helps me track lists and searches. I can also manage multiple Twitter accounts easily. Tweets are threaded, too, so you can easily track the conversations. Normally, you tweet and respond to the replies you receive, but you can't dig back to see how the conversation began. Threaded conversations help you keep track of the full conversation.

Plume

Plume (myplume.com) is among the most popular Android apps for Twitter. You can add multiple Twitter profiles and easily add photos and locations to your tweets. You can also see the conversation thread to keep track of the conversation. Finally, you can access your lists and saved search results quickly.

Tweet-Ups

In Chapter 1, I wrote about an impromptu tweet-up between Scott Monty and me that occurred during the South by Southwest Interactive festival. It was from this experience that I learned the value of tweet-ups. So what exactly is a tweet-up?

Simply put, a *tweet-up* is an in-person meetup with your friends on Twitter. These can be prescheduled large formal events, or simple after work drinks. Schedule a lunch tweet-up in your city, or refuel with your fellow Twitter pals at a local cafe.

I travel from Nashville to Toronto a couple times a year for business and to catch up with my friends and family back home. I always organize a tweet-up while I am in Toronto, so I can meet up with my Twitter friends, clients, and anyone else interested in attending. The events are open to the public, assuming you're on Twitter.

In 2009, I held a tweet-up in Toronto where Merlene Payner and Randy Mattheson attended. They didn't know each other, aside from on Twitter, of course. It was from meeting at my tweet-up that Randy and Merlene became a couple. Each year they remind me of this story, and I'm so thankful that I organized that event. My heart warms just writing this. Networking is about bringing people together. It's about being a connector. Twitter connects.

It amazes me that more businesses don't take advantage of this opportunity to actually meet their customers and potential customers in person.

I used to create tweet-ups when I was attending a conference or event on a company's behalf. I would bring along some swag from the company to give away, and I would buy appetizers and a few rounds of drinks for the attendees. It was always a blast to connect and network with customers and friends. Remember that networking online is wonderful, but the real magic occurs when you meet offline in real life (IRL).

Use Twitter to build your network, but be sure to meet people IRL when you can. In Chapter 9, "If You Build It, They Will Come: Organizing Events," I write at length about the amazing experiences I've had organizing and attending events. Twitter plays an important part of spreading the word for your events, so use it to connect online and offline.

Twitter for Business

Twitter has proven to be a valuable networking tool for me. I've made many good friends and grown my network and business using the microblogging service. It's important to think about how you will use it for yourself and your business or workplace.

Most of the largest brands have profiles on Twitter. Examples are Starbucks @starbucks and Southwest Airlines @southwestair. If you're a small business, it's important to consider if your company should have a Twitter presence. Here are two questions to ask about your company:

1. Will you be able to balance running both a personal Twitter account and a business account? Remember that you're not just pushing out tweets; you're managing relationships, too.

2. What will you tweet from your business account that is different from your personal one? Remember that including personal tweets and promoting others is an important way to grow your network.

Did you decide to create a business profile on Twitter?

When I managed Griffin Technology's social media, I created and managed the @griffintech account myself. I recommend that small to medium sized businesses appoint one person to manage their Twitter account if possible. For companies that are using a single person to manage their Twitter account, I recommend you do so in the following way: Use a Twitter profile picture that is a good headshot of yourself. Then include a small logo from your company in the image. People prefer to communicate with a person over a logo. It adds personality and trust.

If you are a large company, you might have a team who runs your Twitter account and decides to use your logo as your Twitter profile picture. Share the people behind the tweets by using their initials at the end of each tweet. Create a custom

background image that includes their names, photos, initials (to put a face to the tweet), and anything else. Blackberry (https://twitter.com/@blackberry) and Aetna's customer service department (https://twitter.com/@AetnaHelp) are great examples. You may even choose to create a bio page on your site featuring your Twitter team. Include a link to this in your bio so that followers can click through to learn more. Alternatively, you can choose to include your Twitter team's personal handles in your corporate bio.

At Griffin, I included my full name in my Twitter profile bio, so anyone interested would know who I was. If you're representing your company, you should be proud to share your photo and name. When I would attend conferences and events, people would recognize me by my picture and say, "Hi Dave!" before I could introduce myself.

If you have a good exchange with a person representing a brand on Twitter, you are more likely to choose her product over a competitor's. By having a true interaction with a brand representative on Twitter, you establish a real relationship. The more conversations that occur, the closer that relationship becomes. Not everybody wants to be a brand's best friend on Twitter, but being there to listen, answer questions, and help customers is key. Ultimately, I wanted customers to choose a Griffin product over a competitor's because of the interactions they had with me.

Regardless of whether you decide to represent your company from your personal Twitter profile or your company Twitter profile, it's important to be human, casual, and humorous. Avoid constantly promoting your own products or services, coupons, and contests. These are all great things to share, but be sure to spend the majority of the time interacting with your followers and sharing great content like interesting stories and blog posts; listening and responding quickly to tweets referencing you, your products, or the company you work for; and sharing personal anecdotes.

Connecting from a 1972 VW Bus

In December 2009, four colleagues at Griffin and I embarked on a 2,500 mile journey from Nashville, TN to Las Vegas for the Consumer Electronics Show (CES). Our departure from Nashville coincided with Griffin's new brand logo and look. The story was much bigger than just a road trip, because we bought the 1972 VW Westfalia bus during the summer and spent countless hours after work and on weekends restoring it and preparing it for the journey.

Twitter played a major role on our road trip and during the bus restoration. I used a unique Twitter account called @cesbound instead of Griffin's regular @griffintech. The @cesbound tweets were all related to the state of the bus (affectionately known as "Double Nickels") and to connect with our followers along the way.

I organized tweet-ups in New Orleans, Austin, Phoenix, and Las Vegas before our departure, to network with our customers in person. It was such a pleasure making new friends and connecting with them in person. We also brought plenty of great Griffin gear and custom CES Bound t-shirts to give away. Twitter was crucial in communicating with our customers before, during, and after the trip concluded. The journey not only grew our network, but it left us with new friends, too. You can view the photos from the tweet-ups and more at http://bit.ly/cesboundphotos. Double Nickels now resides in Griffin's lobby at their headquarters in Nashville.

Think of creative ways to use Twitter to create a buzz, engage with your customers, and build relationships and your network.

Think Before You Tweet

I have to say it: Think before you tweet. If you manage more than one Twitter account, always check which Twitter account you're tweeting from. Accidents happen, and tweets fueled by bad judgment occur, but they shouldn't. I've seen people who have accidentally tweeted negative tweets from company profiles. Think before you tweet.

If you're angry, wait before you publish the tweet. The same can be said for anything you publish online, including email. Not only can a bad tweet make you lose followers, it can also make you lose clients and job prospects. I grappled with the idea of using this portion of the chapter to share horror stories, but I would prefer to warn you than to shame people.

Tweets can be deleted, but that doesn't mean they're permanently removed. The same goes for anything you put online. There's even a site dedicated to collecting embarrassing deleted tweets. Be careful.

Think Before You Let Others Tweet for You

I strongly believe that Twitter is about building relationships and ultimately a strong network. This means that only you should run your personal profile. You can talk about your business, but remember not to be too self-promotional.

Businesses sometimes hire agencies or their interns to tweet on their behalf. I'm not fond of this idea for several reasons. Just as I stated throughout this chapter, Twitter is about building relationships and networking. Smart businesses interact with their customers regularly. Interns can't always speak with full knowledge of the company, its products, and services. Agencies can push promotional offers and reply to tweets, but when someone follows up with you after meeting at a conference, he won't be remembered by an agency.

Say Hello

Twitter is a wonderful way to connect and meet people who have similar interests to you. By providing inspirational, informative, advocating, and entertaining tweets, you gain followers and grow your network.

Don't be overwhelmed or obsessed with your number of followers. Remember that quality matters over quantity. Many of my friends are ones I first met on Twitter. By meeting people and participating in the conversations, you will have good Twitter friends of your own in little time. You can begin the process by taking a break now, logging into Twitter, and saying hello directly to me @davedelaney. I look forward to hearing from you.

Endnotes

1. www.statista.com/statistics/191952/percentage-of-us-americans-who-are-aware-of-twitter-since-2008/

2. http://articles.washingtonpost.com/2012-07-30/business/35488395_1_public-tweets-twitter-users-user-mark

3. www.chrisbrogan.com/how-to-manage-twitter/

4. www.mediabistro.com/alltwitter/500-million-registered-users_b18842

5. www.nytimes.com/2009/09/09/dining/09pour.html?_r=1

6. https://twitter.com/chrismessina/status/223115412

6

One Billion People Can't Be Wrong: Facebook

Let's face it: You're on Facebook, as are your mother, your grandfather, and your kids. As of October 2012, one billion monthly active users[1] are on the wildly popular social networking site. Compare this to LinkedIn's 187 million members[2] to consider why you should also use Facebook to connect and grow your network.

Facebook users are older than you think. Sixty-five percent of users in the United States are 35 years old or older.[3] In fact, the average age of a Facebook user in the United States is 40.5 years old, with studies indicating similar numbers in different countries.[4]

If 66% percent of online adults say they use Facebook,[5] and the average user is 40.5 years old, you can bet there are professional opportunities for you. In this chapter, I will write about how best to use Facebook to grow your professional relationships and strengthen your career.

Your Profile

Before you head out to a networking event, job interview, or client meeting, you will likely choose something tasteful to wear, put on some makeup, shave, fix your hair, and get ready to impress. We do this to make a good impression.

Too many people use Facebook to post embarrassing photos of themselves. It's as if nobody is looking, right? However, the people that we dress up to impress may very well decide to visit your Facebook profile to learn more about you. All the hairspray, shaving cream, and dapper duds won't do you a lick of good once a potential employer has seen you wearing a hard hat with a beer can affixed to each side.

Consider this when posting photos to your profile. Maybe the embarrassing shots can be reserved for...nowhere! Remember never to put something online you wouldn't want your mother to see.

 Tip

You're only permitted one personal Facebook profile. Use your real name, and don't create a business profile. Businesses should have a page instead.

During presidential elections, there's plenty of colorful commentary from overly passionate people about their favorite (and least favorite) political party and politician. I would be willing to bet that many opportunities are lost because someone posted something offensive or left a comment in the heat of the moment.

You can stop here for a moment and look at your public Facebook profile. To do this, you need to take note of your Facebook username. Click your name in the top-left corner of your profile and take note of the URL at the top of the page. My personal profile is facebook.com/dave.delaney, but yours may have a mix of random numbers.

 Tip

To choose a better Facebook URL (by removing the random numbers), go to your Account Settings and select Username. Be sure to use your real name, and note that you can only change your username once. If you have a common name, you may have to get creative and use your initials instead like "d.delaney" or "daveadelaney".

Log out of Facebook and visit your profile's URL to see what information you have accessible to the public. What does it tell me about you? Does it relay the person you want to share with the world? I'll talk more about privacy settings and permissions in this chapter.

Please don't misunderstand; you can have fun on Facebook. I'm not a stick in the mud. Just try not to get too carried away by oversharing information that others may be troubled by or content that makes you look unprofessional. Facebook is certainly fun, but it's fun in public, so keep that in mind.

What Your About Section Tells Me

What does your About section (like your bio) say about you on Facebook? Just like your LinkedIn profile, it's important to keep your place of employment and contact information up to date on your About section. Don't forget to add a link to your splash page or blog. Give a visitor somewhere else to go to learn more about you beyond Facebook.

What Are You Sharing?

If you work as a financial advisor, I would expect some of your content on your Facebook profile to include links and commentary about the industry. This doesn't mean that you have to bore the pants off your friends and family, but they probably respect you and appreciate your thoughts. That's my point: What are you sharing on Facebook?

If you followed my steps in Chapter 3, "Your Home on the Web Needs More Than a Welcome Mat," and created a blog, Facebook is ideal for sharing the content you create there. Don't overshare your own work. This can annoy your friends, but you *should* promote your best work. Use your profile to share your favorite peer work, too. Your network will be much healthier if you use your profile to promote their content, too.

Friend Requests

Facebook is all about connecting and growing relationships. It's social networking to the core. This means that you're expected to send friend requests. You probably already have sent a few of your own when you created your profile. If not, the steps are as simple as setting up your Twitter and LinkedIn profiles. By giving Facebook access to your email address book, Facebook can automatically find your contacts who are already Facebook users. Go ahead and get *friending*. Choose valuable people to add to your personal network.

Visit Facebook.com/friends and click the Find Friends button in the top-right corner. Doing so reveals several smart recommendations for you to get started searching for people you know.

Search by your hometown or current city. Choose classmates from college or graduate school. In some cases you may want to select friends from high school, too. You may want to review what they're doing now before sending the request. The last thing you want is to be flooded with odd comments, terrible photos, and game requests from that weird guy from chemistry class.

Use Mutual Friend to find connections you may have to someone you want to get to know better. For example, you may want to get to know a business owner you want to work for. You can search the owner's friends to see who you may know. This is similar to how you find connections on LinkedIn.

The Employer option is another great way to find influencers you should consider adding to your personal network. For example, you can search for local reporters by their publication or investors by their firms. Only connect with people you've met, though. If you're a business owner, use this to also connect with your staff if you feel it's appropriate. Note that former employees will also be included in the results of your search, so take note of their job title before sending the request.

 Caution

Send requests sparingly. Facebook's algorithm detects if you send too many failed requests. Facebook recommends that you send friend requests only to people you have a "real-life connection to."[6]

Facebook marketing expert and author Mari Smith has written that she uses her personal profile to friend influential people. Mari connects with people in related industries where she sees an opportunity to help them or for them to help her. Of course, she also connects with friends and family, but she does her best to use Facebook to "educate and inform."[7] This is a smart approach, because her network of Facebook friends then recognizes her as an expert. You can imagine the referrals she gets from such a smart strategy.

 Caution

It's important to understand that it's against Facebook's Terms of Service to use your profile exclusively for business promotion. You can have your profile taken down by Facebook for breaking the rules. Use Facebook Pages for the bulk of the business.

Don't Abuse Your Friends

Just because someone has accepted you as a friend doesn't mean you can start posting special offers or links to your company on her wall. This is a *huge* no-no.

The same goes for tagging a friend in a post that you write just so the friend sees it. Don't do this.

Just as you would behave at a networking event, don't start selling yourself or your products as soon as someone accepts your friend request. How about a quick note to say hello and thanks? Maybe even ask your new friend a question about sports or movies or life in general. You get the idea.

Privacy Settings and Tips

Facebook and privacy settings have a bit of a checkered past. Settings and functionality change from time to time, so it's important to be familiar with the most current format.

Begin by clicking the gear icon at the top right next to your name. Select Privacy Settings. Click the Edit button next to "Who can see my stuff?" The following options will appear:

- **Public**—Everyone will see your posts.
- **Friends**—Only your friends will see your posts.
- **Friends except Acquaintances**—Acquaintances are friends you don't keep in touch with. You can add them to this list and not see them appear in your newsfeed very often.
- **Only Me**—You.
- **Custom**—You can create even smaller segments here. For example, you may choose to just share with specific friends or lists. You can also exclude people here or lists if you prefer. (More on lists later in this chapter.)

If you want to be a networking powerhouse on Facebook, you should try to be as open as possible. In this case, you would select Public.

Custom settings have several different options you may want to consider, though. You can make your regular posts visible to just your Friends, your Friends of Friends, Specific People, or Specific Lists.

An interesting idea is to use the Hide This From option and select a list of people you definitely don't want to see all your silly status updates.

Scroll down the page under the three types of privacy settings, and you'll find How to Connect. I select Public for all my settings. This way I can be easily found, and people can send me friend requests.

 Note

If you become a Facebook networking black belt, 5,000 friends is your limit. Sorry, but Facebook won't let you have more. Still, it's quality over quantity. Remember this.

The Timeline and Tagging section is important. Be sure to review the settings on each section. Here you can control who can post items on your timeline. You can review posts, photos, and videos you are tagged in before they appear. You can also control who can see the items you are tagged in.

Use "Who can post on your timeline?" to keep control of the content that appears on your timeline. I recommend you enable the option to "Review posts friends tag you in before they appear on your timeline." This will prevent those unwanted college photos from appearing on your profile. Remember that potential customers and recruiters will review your Facebook profile. Be sure you are in control of it.

You should also visit the Apps section of your profile from time to time to review which applications you have granted access to your profile. Remove the old apps you no longer use.

Liking Brands

By liking brand pages, you're sharing your support or interest in them with your friends and profile visitors (if this is visible). I can't lie and say I haven't liked a legitimate brand's page to be entered to win an exotic holiday. Who couldn't use an exotic holiday? Still, the bulk of the pages you like should be brands that you can advocate for.

Facebook's advertising system can pull your profile and feature it in an ad for a brand you have liked to your friends. Think carefully before you like a brand that you may not want to be publicly associated with.

Ninety percent of recruiters and hiring managers visit a potential candidate's profiles on social networks as part of the screening process.[8] I would expect that they review the pages that candidates like on Facebook, so keep this in mind as you click the Like button.

When you're writing a post about a reputable brand, be sure you always tag the name of the page so the company is notified. This is something I'm surprised more

people don't do. To tag, use the @ symbol followed by the company name (or page name). Why not let the company know that you have something great to say? This can get you on the company's radar as a potential candidate for a position; anything is possible. The company may also choose to like or reply to your comment. This is a good opportunity to open a dialogue and learn more about the company.

Interest Lists

When logged in to your profile page on Facebook, you'll notice a section on the left side near the bottom of the page titled Interests. The Interests section of Facebook is a great one that some people miss. You can subscribe to lists dedicated to categories you're interested in, such as Tech Science, Innovative Brands, Advertising, and so on. You can subscribe to these interest lists to stay abreast of new trends in your field of expertise. By sharing the content you find relevant, you remind your friends of your line of work. Consider creating your own list and sharing it with your friends.

Smart Lists

With Smart Lists, you can create specific lists of people you want to share items with. For example, not everyone in your network wants to see your countless baby pictures. Instead, you can choose to just share the photos or posts with a select group of people.

Facebook breaks down its Smart List feature to three types:

- **Close Friends**—Your best friends who should show up more in the news feed.
- **Acquaintances**—Friends who should show up less in the news feed.
- **Restricted**—Friends who can only see posts and profile info you make public.

Facebook also takes the information you provide to produce several additional helpful lists:

- **Employment**—Friends and fellow employees that you work with.
- **School**—Friends you went to school with.
- **City**—Friends located in the same city as you.
- **Family**—Your family, of course.

When you're about to publish a status update, you may choose to share it only with a certain list by clicking the Public tab below the field. This is a perfect way to only share more personal content with your closest friends and family.

Just because you choose to share a private update with a particular list doesn't mean it won't be shared elsewhere. For example, somebody could take a screen capture of your post and share it elsewhere on the Web. Keep this in mind.

Company Smart Lists

I spoke with a number of friends about Company Smart Lists on Facebook recently, and they were all surprised that this feature existed. By selecting your company or even a previous employer that you have included in your About section, you can see all staff members updates in the list. This is a great way to keep up with your colleagues and strengthen those relationships.

To access these company lists, visit: https://www.facebook.com/bookmarks/lists.

Groups

According to a February 2010 article from AllFacebook.com, Facebook could have as many as 620 million Facebook groups.[9] Based on that number and that several years have passed, it's safe to assume that there is a ginormous number of groups available for you to join. Yes, that's right. I used the word *ginormous*.

I love Facebook groups because they provide you with the information and connections from the right people you want to hear from. Like LinkedIn, you can search for groups by interest and request to join them to participate in the conversations around certain topics. This is Facebook networking at its finest.

When you look at the Groups section of your profile, Facebook provides a list of suggested groups on the right side of the page. Be sure to choose See All to get a comprehensive look. You will also get to see which of your friends are already members of these groups.

Once you're a member, spend time networking by answering questions and adding to the discussions. Just like at a networking event, if you spend your time alone there, what fun is that? Mingle!

If you develop a good rapport with members of the group, be sure to send them a friend request.

You can join no more than 300 groups per a Facebook limitation. However, I recommend you join only a handful of groups. Groups are most useful when you participate in them. I don't think I know anyone who has the free time to be active in 300 groups. If they do, they should probably get out more. Remember, networking is about building true relationships with like-minded people or those with similar interests. It is not a "whoever has the biggest number wins" game.

Creating a Group

Creating and leading your own group is a terrific way to foster community. You run the show, so lead the conversations and share your expertise with the group. Encourage interactions, and promote those who are most active. Being a leader is a good way to grow your network, because members will want to be directly connected with you. It's simple to set up a group. Begin by visiting Facebook.com/about/groups/.

Select your group name, and invite a couple of close contacts at first. Consider which type of group you want to create; each has pluses and minuses.

Secret

Only your members will be able to see who and what is in your secret group. This is a good idea if you want to privately share discussions about topics you don't want to share with the world. Membership is by invitation only. A secret group is handy for staff only, a club, or a private peer networking group.

Closed

Your closed group is visible across Facebook. Visitors can see who is in the group, but they can't see what's being posted there. This is a good solution to create some buzz about your group to make people really want to become a member. You can also use it to carefully vet the types of members. For example, perhaps you only want to provide a space for real estate agents to network together.

Open

Your public group is open for the world to see. Facebook members can see who belongs to the group and what's being discussed there. If you're trying to build a big network, a public group will help you achieve this by letting anyone join. You can also encourage your members to promote the group to their friends.

I'm a member of each type of group. I enjoy my professional conversations about industry-related topics by smart people in several secret and closed groups. I'm also a member of some fun public groups where I've met a lot of great new friends.

Decide which type of group meets your needs, and more importantly, the needs of your community.

Happy Birthday!

Let's go ahead and agree that managing hundreds or thousands of relationships is impossible. By creating Facebook lists as I have previously outlined, you can keep track of the people closest to you. But what about everyone else?

One feature of Facebook that I absolutely love is birthdays. Each day that I log in to Facebook, I take note of friends' birthdays. I do my best to visit their profile to wish them a happy birthday, but I also take note of what they're doing. Have they changed jobs? Did they have any other life events recently that I might have missed?

Use Facebook birthdays as a reminder to reach out and touch base with an old friend you haven't spoken to in a while. If you see that your friend is between jobs, it would be a great opportunity to offer to help her. For example, you could ask what companies your friend would like to work with. Check Facebook and LinkedIn to see if you have a contact you can connect your friend with. Or maybe the friend has a product or service that is suitable for your company. Why not set up a call for a demo?

You might use Facebook birthdays as a way to weed out people you accidentally accepted friend requests from. Unfortunately, spammers are everywhere online. They even send you friend requests from time to time. If you see a birthday from a suspicious person, perhaps it is time to unfriend him.

Want to take Facebook birthdays to a whole other level and super-charge your networking efforts? Send your contact an actual birthday card—in the mail. There's something special these days in receiving tangible items when we spend so much of our time balancing relationships online. I don't recommend you send every contact a birthday card, but you could do it for closer friends and acquaintances. Take note of their employer listed in their About section, and send the card to the office.

I recommend that you export your friends' Facebook birthdays and import them into Apple iCal, Microsoft Outlook, or Google Calendar. This way you'll have a clear look ahead at whose birthday is coming up.

In your Facebook profile, select Events from the left side. Click Birthdays at the bottom of the Events section, and choose Export Birthdays at the bottom of the page. Then import the file into the calendar software of your choice.

Not only is it good to be reminded of your friends' birthdays coming up, but it's good to be reminded of who you're connected with on Facebook. When you add hundreds or thousands of people as friends, it's hard to keep track of who all of them are. Facebook birthdays serve as a good way to keep up and a great excuse to reach out to see how they are doing and wish them a happy birthday.

Follow

Become a thought leader in your industry by sharing relevant content that people will be interested in. Then let others follow you to subscribe to the great content you share. Facebook's Follow feature is available at: https://www.facebook.com/about/follow.

Followers are different from friends, because they don't have to send you a friend request to see your updates. You can select which updates you want to share with your followers. Having a large number of followers makes you stand out as a thought leader. For example, Robert Scoble is a well-known technology reporter and author who has nearly 500,000 followers of his Facebook profile. He's a great resource for anyone interested in emerging technologies.

You should also follow people you want to learn more from and perhaps connect with later. The key thing with following Facebook users is that you don't have to be friends with them (or vice versa). You might not personally know thought leaders in your industry, but by following, you can still learn from them.

To set up your profile to allow followers, click the arrow on the gear icon on the top-right side of your screen. On the left side, choose Followers. Be sure to check out the preview and click the link at the bottom titled "Want to Know What Your Followers Can See? View Your Public Timeline." It's wise to review how your public profile appears to potential employers or clients.

Photos Albums

I've mentioned multiple times that you should avoid sharing less than charming photos of yourself. Did you know that you can set the privacy settings on each of your photo albums? Don't forget to tag your friends in decent photos. You can also tag brands with pages, such as a conference you attended or a company event. Include the location of the photos so they appear in the results of the venue's Facebook page. By sharing photos, you encourage people to interact with them from likes and shares to comments. Take a look at the profiles of the people who are commenting, reply to those comments, and start a conversation. Networking is about connecting, right?

Growing Your Network

Assuming you've made some changes to spruce up your Facebook profile, now it's time to add more friends. Remember to choose them wisely.

Networking Apps

As of April 2012, there were 9 million apps[10] (applications) available for Facebook. These apps range widely across many categories, and a few are specific to networking and careers. I recommend avoiding the game apps if you can. If you can't, be sure to limit how they reach (and ultimately annoy) your friends.

The following are a few apps worth considering for your networking efforts.

BranchOut

"BranchOut helps you expand your career network to include your professional friends on Facebook." Go to apps.facebook.com/branchout/.

I like BranchOut's search functionality. You can search for a job title or company and find out who you're connected to on Facebook. This can be handy to get introductions at companies or to make introductions to help members of your network.

BeKnown by Monster

"Now you can connect professionally on Facebook without mixing business and friends." Find it at apps.facebook.com/beknown/.

I like the way BeKnown ties in Monster.com's large database of open positions. By integrating with your Facebook contacts, it helps to get you introductions.

By installing the application, you turn your Facebook network into opportunities for employment. Once connected, you can use Monster.com and search for open positions as normal, but you will have the added advantage of seeing who you know among your Facebook friends that work with the company.

Talent.Me

"Build your personal brand. Get opportunities. Connect with Facebook. Get Endorsed. Receive endorsements from friends and co-workers for specific talents." Talent.Me is at apps.facebook.com/talentme/.

Once connected to Facebook, visit http://www.talent.me and find your Facebook friends. From here, you can search companies you are interested in and find open job listings. Talent.Me reminds me of LinkedIn, because it encourages you to give and receive endorsements. These endorsements will appear on talent.me and your Facebook profile

Glassdoor

"Search jobs then look inside. Company salaries, reviews, interview questions, and more—all posted anonymously by employees and job seekers." Download this app from www.glassdoor.com/.

While Glassdoor is not necessarily a Facebook application, it is a valuable tool for people trying to learn about jobs and companies. Interested in getting your foot in the door at a company? Use Glassdoor to see if any of your Facebook friends are connected to anyone at the company. Glassdoor also provides information about company culture and salaries.

Facebook for Business

An important note about using your personal Facebook profile for business efforts: Do so sparingly. Use it to remind your friends what you do for a living or what kind of employment you're seeking. Don't use it to overly promote your products or services. If you want to promote a business, do so with a Facebook page. You can also promote your Facebook page content *occasionally* on your personal Facebook profile.

Call it ironic, but I decided to ask a question on LinkedIn to see what success people have had in professional networking on Facebook. The majority of the answers were positive. Here are some of the best ones:

> "I found my current freelance writing opportunity through my personal Facebook profile. Connections are truly important! While FB is primarily for family and friends, I try to keep my comments neutral because you never know who is reading. It's always a good idea to present yourself well at all times and on all platforms."

> "Yes, fabulous marketing coaching and training clients have found me there via my updates."

> "Yes, of course. Facebook is a coming together of people. If you use it only to share personal info with family and friends, then that's what you'll get. But if you open it up to other people and possibilities, it is nothing more than another way to connect. To say that only LinkedIn can be used for business is like saying only business networking events can lead to business opportunities, but not a social event."

> "I am currently discussing a fairly significant training project with a great, high profile client—that came through a Facebook friend. That friend was a business connection I made several years ago. We connected on Facebook, and now it's led to this. I have many business "friends" on Facebook, in addition to my social friends and family."

"It's all about how you approach it. Today, ANY opportunity to connect and share is an opportunity to give and receive value."

"Your friends are your advocates. If your friends won't refer you to potential customers, it's going to be a long road ahead. The long and short of it all, yes, I share my business promotions, blog posts, and successes with all of my social media profiles...especially my personal Facebook."

Facebook Pages

Networking is about building relationships, not just selling your wares. A Facebook page is an essential place for most businesses today, so it makes sense to create a page to support your business or the company you work for.

Take some time to set some goals for your Facebook page. Write down what you hope to achieve launching a Facebook page. Ultimately, your Facebook page should be an extension of you or your business. Use it to grow your fan base by increasing page likes, but think carefully about what you will share on your page and how you hope your fans will interact with you there. Be sure to use it to interact with your fans, too. I will speak more to tracking your Facebook page successes later in the chapter.

Some company pages support local charities and match $1.00 for each new like they receive. This is a clever way to help your community, do good will, increase fans, and support a good cause.

United Airlines Mileage Plus did a wonderful job giving away 10 million free miles to charities involved. Participants could vote on their favorite charity which would receive additional miles to the 25,000 each was initially rewarded (Figure 6.1).

This promotion engaged United's existing customers and potential customers in its philanthropic efforts. Not only did this give United's brand a positive image, it helped strengthen United's relationships with its customers and helped set United apart from its competitors.

Figure 6.1   *United Airlines 10 Million Charity Miles Giveaway.*[11]

Creating a Facebook Page

If Facebook were a country, it would be the third largest after India and China.[12] In 2013, most small business owners should consider having a presence on the world's largest social networking site. There are already approximately 42 million Facebook pages,[13] and this number does not seem to be slowing.

For the purposes of New Business Networking, there are two main reasons why someone would start a Facebook page. They reached the maximum 5,000 friends that Facebook allows for a personal account, or they have a company or brand that needs a presence.

Use your personal profile to build relationships and to share personal and business-related content. Primarily focus on business topics when using a Facebook page, but share a behind-the-scenes look at your coworkers (with their permission, of course) and office, too. Consider spotlighting your customers and other local businesses you enjoy.

People stress about the number of likes their Facebook page has. In John Morgan's book *Brand Against the Machine*, he reminds his readers that "a hundred fully engaged fans are better than a thousand unengaged fans." I couldn't agree more.

You want to increase the number of likes you have. Who doesn't? Still, it's more important that you have fans who care and interact with you on your page.

By visiting www.facebook.com/pages, you can set up your own page and tweak it until your heart is content before making it public. Have fun designing the look and feel of your thumbnail photo and your timeline cover image.

Note the different categories you can choose from to make your page: Local Business or Place; Company, Organization or Institution; Brand or Product; Artist, Band, or Public Figure; Entertainment; Cause or Community.

I recommend that you add another admin to your page. This is important should you ever be unable to access your Facebook account. It's crucial that somebody can manage it for you in your absence.

Follow the Rules

Facebook has terms of use for everything you do there, but the rules are more strict on Facebook pages. For example, your timeline image can't have a call to action, meaning it can't include a phone number or a Like Us message.

Facebook page terms change pretty frequently, so be sure you visit www.facebook. com/page_guidelines.php and familiarize yourself with the most up-to-date rules of the game.

Facebook Page Tips

Use your Facebook page to grow your network by sharing interesting content and promotions that your fans will enjoy and avoid constantly selling to them. Selling too much will only result in unlikes. Instead, consider how you can help your fans. Social networking is all about being social. This means you should be interacting with your Facebook page fans several times a day if possible. Interact regularly, and share great content like links to interesting stories or thought-provoking posts.

When a fan interacts with you, don't miss your opportunity to connect. Be present and respond promptly. This may include liking a fan's comment or replying to her comment. Avoid Yes/No replies. Perhaps you can continue the conversation with a question.

Facebook is open 24 hours a day, 7 days a week. Use several short blocks of time to interact daily, including weekends. In some cases, weekends are actually busier for Facebook pages.

Use a line at the bank, grocery store, or school pickup to check your Facebook page on your smart phone. You can do this using Facebook's standard app, but I also recommend that you download and install the Facebook Pages Manager app available in your mobile devices app store.

By regularly asking questions, you are sure to get a good response and increased engagement on your page. The more people who interact with you, the more likely they will share their participation with friends outside of your page. This can equal new fans quickly.

Post photos on your Facebook page. Using a behind-the-scenes photo each day or once a week requesting captions from your fans is a great way to increase engagement. It's also fun to see what people come up with. Don't forget to like their captions and comment where applicable.

Occasional videos are also a fun way to share what's on your mind. Consider making one to introduce yourself to new fans who may not know you and your company or place of employment well yet. Ask a question and encourage comments.

Don't forget to let your Facebook friends know about your Facebook page. Invite them to join you there and tell them why. For example, if you're a photographer, you should tell your friends that you plan to share more photos and contests on your page more frequently than your personal profile. You can set up a poll to have your fans vote on their favorite photos.

You can also invite new fans by linking to your Facebook page on your splash page, blog, in a blog post, in your email signature, and occasionally on your other social sites like Twitter, LinkedIn, and Google+.

Facebook Insights

The Insights section of your page gives you an overview of its performance. Key metrics include Total Likes, Friends of Fans, People Talking About This, and Weekly Total Reach. As you dig a little deeper, you can see demographics and location information about your page fans.

Facebook describes the following:

- **Total Likes**—The number of unique people who like your page.
- **Friends of Fans**—The number of unique people who are friends with people who have liked your page.
- **People Talking About This**—The number of unique people who have created a "story" from your post. This includes actions like liking your page or a post, commenting, sharing, answering your questions, sharing your page, and more. This shows the activity taking place on your page.
- **Weekly Total Reach**—The number of unique people who have seen any content associated with your page.

Use these numbers to get a better understanding of the performance of your page and record your findings in a spreadsheet. Facebook shows you key metrics from 28 days, so it's best to do your report every 28 days.

Create a column in your spreadsheet to keep track of each number. Include a section to track the most popular posts on your page. This can reveal insight like whether your fans prefer interacting with questions, longer commentary, or photos.

Page Posts

The Page Posts section reveals figures such as Reach, Engaged Users, Talking About This, and Virality as it is related specifically to the content you post on your Facebook page.

Facebook describes the following:

- **Reach**—The number of unique people who have seen your post.
- **Engaged Users**—The number of unique people who have clicked on your post.
- **Talking About This**—The number of unique people who have created a story about the post (described previously).
- **Virality**—The percentage of people who have created a story from your page post out of the total number of unique people who have seen it.

Again, I encourage you to share your original content such as your blog posts on your page. Using Google Analytics, you can measure the traffic coming from Facebook back to your site. This is an important metric to measure as well.

Every 28 days, you should do your best to add the most recent data. Over time you will begin to gauge what's working best and what's not. Don't obsess about these numbers, but use them to lead you to informed decisions.

Facebook EdgeRank

Facebook's mysterious algorithm is called EdgeRank. It's Facebook's secret recipe and the robot brains behind the social network. Just as KFC has its famous eleven herbs and spices, Facebook has its secret ingredients, too. The difference with KFC is that Facebook changes the recipe from time to time.

EdgeRank automatically chooses which items should appear in your News Feed. EdgeRank protects you from spam infiltrating, and its goal is to make the most relevant content get to you first.

Nobody fully understands EdgeRank. If they did, it would already be changed. What's clear is that content that resonates with your audience performs better than poor content. It's about quality over quantity. By referring to your stats every 28 days, you learn the types of content your fans enjoy most.

Facebook Ads

When I speak with companies who are unsatisfied with Facebook ads, they're usually making one big mistake. They're thinking of Facebook ads like traditional advertising. But Facebook ads are really meticulously targeted marketing messages in the form of ads.

People often try to create an ad that reaches as many people as possible. Are you in New York City? Let's make an ad to reach everyone in NYC! This approach simply won't work. The beauty of Facebook ads is the ability to drill down to exactly the type of people you hope see your ads.

You can use Facebook ads to target the specific market of people you actually want to reach. Instead of everyone in NYC, why not target women in Brooklyn, between 18 and 34, who are married college graduates, who are fans of Etsy and Starbucks, and who are already connected to someone who likes your page?

Take a moment to jot down who you most want to visit and like your page. Where do they live? What age are they? What sex? What interests do they have?

The important thing with Facebook advertisements is to have at least two different ads running at any given time. Advertising (in any medium) is not an exact science. By running multiple ads, you can determine which is working best.

As you use Facebook's advanced targeting, you will discover great ways to reach exactly who you are seeking. I have had great success in using this methodology in providing advertisements for clients.

Check your ads each day to review their performance, and adjust them as needed.

Promoted Posts

A good way to help a post on your Facebook page get more views is to use Facebook's Promoted Posts service. Under each recent post is an option to promote it. Click the drop-down menu to choose a budget and payment option. This is necessary to receive maximum reach for your posts. Choose Promoted Posts for the content that you want to share with the greatest number of people.

Apps for Your Page

There are thousands of Facebook apps for pages. Each application can offer ways to enhance the look and functionality of your page. However, some can cause more trouble than they're worth. Read the reviews and determine which apps best suit your needs.

Consider your fans and what would help make a better experience for them. A musician will choose different apps than a printing company. I've included a few suggestions of apps that I have used and enjoy.

If you have an email newsletter, most email marketing companies have an app that you can install to feature a Sign Up tab on your page. MailChimp is a personal favorite of mine, and it takes just a few steps to install. Once it's installed, a visitor can click the tab and fill out his information to sign up for your newsletter.

OfferPop is a Facebook app development company that offers several great apps for your page. When I had a logo design contest for my monthly cocktail hour, Nashcocktail, I used OfferPop's Tug of War app to put the two most popular logos against one another in a vote. Fans of the Nashcocktail page left comments and voted on their favorite new logo. It was a fun way to bring my network of fans together. Visitors to the page had to like the page before voting, which substantially increased the number of likes to the page. OfferPop has a good selection of other apps worth giving a try.

Remember to have a purpose for your fans using the app. Don't just install apps for the heck of it. Apps can end up cluttering your page and overwhelming your fans with too many options.

I wrote earlier about including photos on your Facebook page. I'll write more about Instagram in Chapter 7, but I recommend that you consider installing the Instagram app so your photos will automatically aggregate to your page. This is a fun way to take the popular photo sharing social network to the next level.

I suggest you visit facebook.com/appcenter/ to review new apps that are available. Avoid the games, and try to find ones that will benefit your fans. AppBistro.com is another good source of applications. Scroll down to select the type of page you administer, and then use the Sort Apps By menu to find the most popular and highly rated apps.

Creative apps can increase interactions on your Facebook page, resulting in more engaged fans. This in turn can result in stronger relationships with your fans.

Grow Your Network Using Facebook

Use your Facebook profile to grow your network of people who can help you and who you can help. This includes your family and friends but should also include people you have met at conferences, events, and in some cases, your customers. Remember not to use your Facebook profile to overly promote yourself or your business. Use it to share anecdotes from work and stories about your business, but don't use it to sell. Be sure you are mixing plenty of personal content, too, because this is your personal profile after all.

Use your Facebook page to promote your business, your fans, and their content. Remember that by sharing other people's work and promoting them, you are networking well. Be sure to use your page to get to know your fans, too. Who are they? What do they do? Ask them how you can help. Share interesting industry-related stories and your blog posts.

It's important to measure your numbers on your page to be sure you're achieving your goals. Don't obsess about metrics, though. It's the genuine interactions and real relationships that matter most.

Advertising is a viable way to promote your page and posts. Constantly test different target markets and advertisement formats. Don't be discouraged if you don't see a huge increase in likes, comments, or shares. Instead, reevaluate the ads and reconfigure them to try again. Be patient.

Facebook is a highly individualized platform that should reflect your or a business's unique personality. Revisit Facebook's Terms of Service from time to time to be sure you are following guidelines correctly. The worst thing that can happen is to have your profile banned or your page taken down. All the time and money you will have invested will be worthless.

I recommend Brian Carter's book *The Like Economy*. Brian has covered much more ground than I possibly could in just one chapter. Facebook is a behemoth, and it's changing frequently. Facebook news sites like insidefacebook.com and allfacebook.com are good sources to follow daily news.

For the purposes of *New Business Networking*, I want you to consider the options I've shared with you about how you can grow your network on Facebook using your profile or page.

Endnotes

1. http://newsroom.fb.com/Key-Facts

2. http://press.linkedin.com/about

3. http://royal.pingdom.com/2012/08/21/report-social-network-demographics-in-2012/

4. http://royal.pingdom.com/2012/08/21/report-social-network-demographics-in-2012/

5. http://pewinternet.org/Commentary/2012/March/Pew-Internet-Social-Networking-full-detail.aspx

6. www.facebook.com/help/240436879374301/

7. www.facebook.com/note.php?note_id=471593071339

8. http://mashable.com/2011/10/23/how-recruiters-use-social-networks-to-screen-candidates-infographic/

9. http://allfacebook.com/google-now-indexes-620-million-facebook-groups_b10520

10. www.insidefacebook.com/2012/04/27/facebook-platform-supports-more-than-42-million-pages-and-9-million-apps/

11. www.10millioncharitymiles.com/

12. http://blogs.wsj.com/digits/2012/04/23/facebook-passes-the-900-million-monthly-users-barrier/

13. www.insidefacebook.com/2012/04/27/facebook-platform-supports-more-than-42-million-pages-and-9-million-apps/

7

Still Growing and One to Watch: Google+

On June 28, 2012, Google introduced its own social network, Google+ (Google Plus). Technology enthusiasts, online marketers, and Google fans scurried to set up an account and test the waters. Today the arguments fly whether Google+ is a place where you want to invest your time and resources. Naysayers call it a "ghost town" and argue that they don't have the time to tend to another social network. However, proponents support Google+ as a strong platform for intelligent discourse and debate.

I think of Google+ as anything but a ghost town, but it's still too early to say with certainty whether it will continue as a social network, or whether it will be amalgamated into Google itself. It is clear that Google hasn't just created another social network—they have created a way to enhance our search results, which is what Google knows best.

Is Google+ for You?

Determining whether Google+ is right for you depends on who you're trying to network with. The majority of people I come across on Google+ are early adopters of new technologies, online marketing professionals, and photographers. Of course, there are many other types of people on Google+. Studies tell a similar story. For example, an article at SocialFresh.com[1] states that Google+ users are most likely students, developers, engineers, designers, and photographers. Flowtown.com reports that 63% of users are male, with the majority being between 24 and 25 years old.[2]

Consider asking your friends, fans, and followers if they're using Google+. Use Facebook, Twitter, or LinkedIn (or all of the above) to get an idea of whether they are using Google+. Doing so will help you decide whether this social network is the right platform for you to reach the people you're trying to network with. If you are a small business owner with a brick and mortar presence, you should definitely use Google+ Local (more on that soon).

Like all networking online and off, always strive to help others before you expect anything in return. Google+ is a good place to share your insights and links to interesting or entertaining content you find and to promote other people and the content they produce. Use Google+ to easily introduce two people; they'll appreciate the new connection. To do this, tag each person in a message introducing them to an article, blog post, or photo.

Nancy VanReece, social media strategist for the Nashville Symphony, does a wonderful job with her personal profile as you see in Figure 7.1. Nancy regularly shares articles about social media marketing, performing arts, and nonprofits. She adds her own commentary and encourages conversation from her network. Nancy specializes in social media marketing for nonprofits and the arts, and she uses Google+ to tell her story, drive conversations, and connect and grow her network.

Ultimately, you must decide whether your target market is already on Google+. If you're a student trying to network to start your career in technology, I highly recommend it. If you're an individual like a photographer who wants to share your work and grow your network, Google+ is an ideal place for you. If you own a local business like a restaurant or hotel, you should consider using it, too.

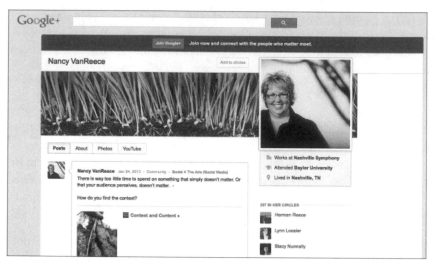

Figure 7.1   *Nancy VanReece.*

It is important to note that Google+ is building its number of users rapidly. If you want to have a good standing within Google's search results, you should consider using Google+. While I may refer to Google+ as another social network (today), it is evolving and becoming more of the overall Google experience—Google is actively amalgamating its other services (like Gmail, YouTube) with Google+. Hence the name of the chapter: "Still Growing and One to Watch."

Getting Started

Setting up your Google+ profile is about as easy as it is on Facebook, LinkedIn, or Twitter. However, you'll need a free Gmail email address to use Google+. Once you have logged in to Gmail, visit plus.google.com to get started.

Use a good headshot. For consistency sake, it's a good idea to use the same photo across all social networks, but this is up to you. Choose a timeline image that complements your profile. Does it tell the visitor a little about you?

Refer to your LinkedIn bio, and create your Google+ bio. Remember that keywords and search terms are important. (Refer to Chapter 4, "Grow Your Network Before You Need It: LinkedIn.") This is Google, after all.

You have an option to import your contacts to Google+ from your email just as you did with the aforementioned social networking sites. Do this so you can instantly see who among your contacts is already a Google+ member. You can also invite people who are not using Google+ yet.

Set up your privacy settings at google.com/settings/u/2/plus. You have options for who sees your updates, photos, and videos. For example, you may want to share your photos and videos only with your family, so set that content with a private Family circle (more on circles in the next section). It's important to remember that the more you make your profile private, the less likely others will be able to find you and get to know more about you. Your life doesn't have to be an open book, but sharing your story will help others connect with you and ultimately grow your network.

When you're configuring your privacy settings, you can select how you're notified of new content and announcements from your contacts, when you are tagged in content (like Facebook), and new requests from people to connect. These push notifications can drive a person a little crazy as your phone vibrates off the table, so decide how and how frequently you want to be alerted.

Circles

Twitter has lists, LinkedIn has groups, and Facebook has groups and lists. To save you any confusion between lists and groups, Google+ has circles. Circles are Google's way for you to categorize your contacts. When you launch your profile, Google+ provides you with a few default circles for you to fill in at will, including Family, Friends, Acquaintances, and Following.

It's dead simple to add people to each circle by a simple drag and drop. You can adjust your preferences for the circles you want to see most frequently. You can also see who among your contacts already has you in their public circles; consider joining them. Take note of the circles your friends and colleagues are members of. This is an excellent starting place to network with other members.

You can search within Google+ to find relevant publicly shared circles you may consider joining. I quite like RecommendedUsers.com to easily search and find people to follow based on categories, as seen in Figure 7.2. For example, you can select Authors & Writers from the navigation to be instantly provided with a list of accomplished professionals.

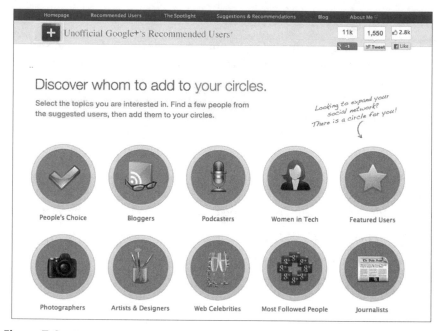

Figure 7.2   *RecommendedUsers.com.*

FindPeopleOnPlus.com is another third-party service worth checking out. This service does a terrific job searching within users' profiles. You can run a search for your university to find classmates, search by location to find people in various cities, or even search for employees within particular companies.

If you want to get to know people at a company for networking purposes, what better way than adding them to a private circle? Search by company name, and select the employees you're interested in following. Add them to a private circle, and refer to it from time to time to interact and get acquainted with them. This sounds sneakier than it is. It works the same way as private Twitter lists and private Facebook lists. You're simply grouping people who you want to get to know better.

Chime in to conversations by commenting and +1 their shared items that you find interesting. If you have a good rapport, invite them for a coffee to learn more about who they are and what they do. Remember that a simple coffee chat can open doors to exciting new opportunities. I've had coffees that have resulted in new clients, new jobs, and new friends. Refer to Chapter 2, "It Starts with a Coffee," if you need a reminder on how best to do this.

Overbearing by Oversharing

The phrase "sharing is caring" is heard time and time again referring to social media. Do your best to share helpful, relevant, and entertaining content with your network. Just a press of the +1 button across the Web, and you automatically share the item on your Google+ profile. This works the same way as the Facebook Like button and the Twitter tweet button. An added benefit to Google+ that is not available to Facebook or Twitter users is the ability to share the item to members of a specific circle instead of sharing it with all of your followers.

On Google+, you have the option of sharing items you find with people. This is perfectly fine to do from time to time, but only when the shared item is relevant to the recipient. Ask yourself the following questions before you hit the Share button:

- Is this item going to help the recipient?
- Is the item relevant to the recipient?
- Have I shared an item with this recipient recently?
- Would I be annoyed if I kept getting items sent to me in the same fashion?

The same rules apply to sharing photos, videos, events, and anything else for that matter. Oversharing borders on spamming. People can remove you from their circles and contacts as easily as they added you.

By all means share. Don't let my words of warning scare you. Do take a moment, though, to consider my questions before you do. You may already know the answer.

Hangouts

The Google+ killer feature is hangouts. By creating a hangout, you can video conference with up to ten people (nine others if you include yourself) at one time. The host of the chat is featured in the top-middle square, and the other participants are in a row of smaller squares below. The clever technology hears who is speaking and moves that person to the top square position, so your eyes naturally focus on the speaker at the top of the screen.

You can also create a hangout with a theme and invite just members of one of your circles. For example, if you have a circle of new contacts you met at a conference, you can invite them to a hangout to discuss what you learned or who your favorite speakers were. Consider the networking potential by reconnecting with the people you briefly met at the conference.

Hangouts work perfectly with YouTube (owned by Google). For example, you could invite a few members of your network or potential customers to view a video together in real time.[3] To do this, choose the "Share" button below any YouTube video. The "Hangout" option will appear, and you will be given options to select who you wish to watch the video with. A request will be sent to your contacts to join the hangout right away. Be sure to use the chat feature so that you can interact with one another as you enjoy the video.

Imagine that you own or work for a small business, like an art supply store or a flower shop. You could send an email newsletter to your customers with a special offer like "Save 50% on Roses" or "Save 25% on Sketching Materials." In addition to this, you could invite customers to join you live on a Google hangout. In this example, I would share a video on how to draw a rose. I use this example because I happened upon a great video on YouTube with nearly 6 million views that walks through the steps.

Together with nine customers, you could interact and get to know each other. When you have completed both the video and your sketches, you could have each person reveal his drawings to the group. This would make for good communal praise or laughing, and your customers would learn something new. The video you watch does not have to be your own. It can be from any user on YouTube. Think about videos your network would enjoy, and invite them to watch one together in real time.

I understand that nine customers may not seem like a large number, but consider the content from such an event. For example, you can write a recap blog post about who participated, what was learned, and include images of your sketches or quotes from some of the participants. Use the blog post to promote your email newsletter so that visitors can sign up to be alerted of your next hangout. If these small training sessions become popular, consider creating your own using Hangouts on Air, which I talk more about in a moment.

Sharing a video in real time is a wonderful way to connect with your network. Rather than airing a self-promotional video, consider sharing a public YouTube video that helps your contacts solve a problem. Here are some more examples:

- **Real Estate Agent**—Could share a video on tips to stage a house.
- **Medical Facility**—Could share a video on how to avoid the flu.
- **Auto Repair Store**—Could share a video on how to change a tire.
- **Clothing Company**—Could show how to accessorize outfits.
- **Web Designer**—Could share a video on how to wireframe a website.

Another idea is to have a free virtual conference. You can choose your favorite presentations on YouTube like TED talks or search for "lectures" and invite your

network to watch the presentations together. You can spend time at the end discussing what you learned, your key takeaways, and your thoughts about the presentations as a whole. This is a good way to engage with your network and to share a conversation about powerful presentations. Virtual conferences are beneficial for both individuals and businesses. If you are new to an industry or looking to grow your network within an industry, conversing with other professionals about a shared topic of interest can be rewarding both intellectually and from a networking standpoint.

Hangouts On Air

On May 7, 2012, Google announced the ability for some users to share live webcasts publicly using Hangouts On Air.[4] Think of this feature as your own personal television channel. There is no maximum number of viewers, because you are streaming live for the world to see.

Your live webcast can be shared on your YouTube channel (I will speak more about YouTube in Chapter 8, "Content Is the Glue That Binds Us Together"), and you can easily embed the show right on your blog or website for your visitors to watch. The show can also be recorded and saved on YouTube if some viewers want to watch it later or you want to archive your episodes.

Online musician promotion company, BandPage, uses Google Hangouts On Air to invite the public to ask questions from successful musicians and music industry professionals. Public guests usually are independent artists trying to learn how to better promote themselves. Take a look at some examples of these at youtube.com/rootmusic.

If you play in a band, you could perform live using Hangouts On Air. At the end of the performance, you could share a link to your PayPal account for virtual tips from the audience. You could also link to a crowd-funding site to help raise money to record an album. You could save the YouTube video and make it unlisted (so the public cannot find it without the link). Then you could share the link with your fans in your email newsletter and invite them to your next scheduled live performance. Or you can make the video public and promote it to your fans hoping they will share it, too.

You can use Hangouts On Air to show a behind-the-scenes look at your business or place of work. Use it to introduce your staff, take questions from your customers, and to show off your state-of-the-art water cooler. These types of peeks behind the curtain humanize your brand, which in turn builds trust. It is much easier to grow your network when members trust you and want to get to know you better. You can show them how you are using Hangouts On Air.

Communities

Google calls its communities feature "a gathering place for your passions."[5] Released in December, 2012, communities gives you the opportunity to create a community group dedicated to a specific topic.

Communities is an excellent way to grow your network by finding people with similar interests. Remember that the more communities you join, the more you need to monitor and participate in discussions, so avoid joining too many at first.

Some popular communities include topics like "Building a Company," "Social Media Professionals," "Web Development," and "Architecture."

If you cannot find a community related to what you do, consider creating your own. By creating a community, you will become a leader and connector and gain respect and acknowledgment from your members. A great bonus to creating a community, rather than simply using a Circle to discuss a topic, is the ability to create subcategories. For example, the WordPress community[6] has Discussion, Developers, Beginners, Available for Work, Post Your Job, WordCamps, Meetups, and Events. Communities also provide you with an About section to briefly describe what your community is about. You can even include community rules you may want to implement so that your members understand the do's and don'ts.

Review my suggestions in Chapter 6, "One Billion People Can't Be Wrong: Facebook," for Facebook group ideas and apply them to Google+ communities. Remember to consider who uses Google+ most and whether your industry peers are there. There is no point in creating a community if nobody is going to participate. Consider asking your classmates, colleagues, or customers to join you.

You also need to decide whether your community is private or public. A public community is probably the best approach, but you may want to reserve a private community for a specific group of peers to discuss a possible project or topic. If you are creating a community for your business, make it public so your customers can find you easily.

Remember that you don't need to create a private community for your friends and family. You can use a private circle like I discussed earlier.

Consider your time that you can allocate in a day to the different groups you join across each social networking site. Facebook has groups, LinkedIn has groups, and Google+ has communities. I encourage you to find groups of people to connect with to help and to grow your network, but watch your clock. You don't have to host your community on your own; you can invite additional moderators to assist you as your community grows.

There are four types of communities you can create. Two are public, and two are private.

- **Public #1**—Anyone can join and post to this community.

  Use this if you want to make an open community that has the most growth potential.

- **Public #2**—Only moderators can post, but anyone can view and add comments.

  This is a good option if you already have a large network that wants to join a community presenting topics and discussions.

- **Private #1**—This is for members only, but content is available from a Google+ search.

  Only members can participate, but the content shared is publicly available.

- **Private #2**—This is for members only, and only those with the community URL can find it.

  Shhh. This secret community is private. Use it for a group that is planning a project together.

One feature I love about communities is the ability to +1 a post anywhere on the Web and share it directly with a specific community without having to visit Google+. Just click the +1 button and scroll down to find the community you want to share it with.

Schedule a hangout with (up to ten) members of your community. Use the live video chat to get to know one another and exchange insights, ask questions, or debate topics.

Be sure to include hashtags in your community posts. The hashtags act as tags, so similar content can be found easily across Google+. For example, clicking "#chiropractic" will reveal other content across Google+ that has the same hashtag.

When you create your community, you have the option to add categories for topics you plan to discuss. I recommend only choosing a handful so your members don't get overwhelmed. Categories help a visitor navigate through the content to pinpoint the specific topic they are interested in and get an idea of the topics discussed.

I highly recommend that you visit www.google.com/+/learnmore/communities to find a community to join and begin to interact with. If you don't see a community on a topic of interest, consider creating your own. You can do so from your personal profile or your company's Google+ page.

Google+ Pages

Just as Facebook pages and LinkedIn pages can be important for your business or employer, Google+ pages can be crucial too. In the first six months of Google+, more than one million businesses established a Google+ page. Today the businesses doing it well are using it to connect directly with their customers by sharing relevant content and interacting using Hangouts On Air, photos, comments, and +1s.

Use your Google+ page similarly to how you use your Facebook page. Share interesting stories, links, and engaging content with your customers and potential customers. Always refrain from being too self-promotional. You may choose to publish content using a service like Hootsuite.com, which can post directly to your Google+ page (and other social profiles), but I prefer to engage directly on the page. I favor this approach because I can be sure it appears how I want it to. For example, if I tag a person or a company, I want to be sure it appears correctly. The same goes for including images or video with a post. In my experience, it is best to use the official method when possible. Encourage your customers to join you on your page.

Do your best to share unique items not shared elsewhere. Hangouts On Air is certainly something not offered by other social networks, for example. Want to see some amazing Google+ Pages for inspiration? Take a look at these sites:

Cadbury UK: https://plus.google.com/+CadburyUK/

Red Bull: https://plus.google.com/+RedBull/

Ford: https://plus.google.com/+ford/

NASA: https://plus.google.com/+NASA/

Google: The World's Largest Search Engine

Don't forget that Google+ is owned by Google. How could you? You can bet that Google is tying its social network into its other applications, and ultimately search results. This means if you want to have a good presence on the world's largest search engine, you'd better be using Google's tools to do so.

A search for "Pottery Barn" at Google.com reveals the usual ads and search results you would expect. However, a glance to the right side of the page shows Pottery Barn's Google+ account in a box (see Figure 7.3).

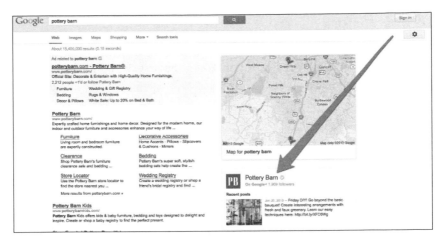

Figure 7.3 *Potterybarn.com.*

The box features a large Follow button, so you can follow Pottery Barn's Google+ page. This is similar to Facebook's brand page Like button. You can also see Pottery Barn's most recent updates on its page and the total number of people who have Pottery Barn in their circles.

Google+ Local

On May 30, 2012, Google launched Google+ Local, a component of Google+ pages. The service allows a user to search for local businesses and find reviews from Zagat, the public, and their friends.

It is best to go ahead and search for your local business to see if you are listed already. If you find your business already listed, you can verify that you own it. Place your mouse over the "unverified" word and choose to "verify now," and then follow the steps to confirm your business address.

Google+ Local takes your local information (address, phone number, location, hours of operation, and so on) and incorporates it with its location-based search results. If I'm hungry and searching for "Italian Restaurant in Houston," chances are likely that those using Google+ Local will be among the top results. The same applies if I search within Google Maps. Google+ Local pulls reviews from Zagat (a popular restaurant review site owned by Google) and from your circles. This combination increases the chances that I will choose your Italian restaurant because of the general decent reviews provided by Zagat and peer reviews from my social contacts. To take a look at Google+ Local businesses, visit: https://plus.google.com/local.

If your business is not yet listed, you should add it. When setting up your Google+ Local information, consider three main points: relevance, distance, and prominence.

- **Relevance**—Be sure you use terms that are specific to your business. In the previous example, you should use "Italian Restaurant," "pizza," "lasagna," "Naples," "Napoli," or "Houston" in the description of your restaurant. Capisce?

- **Distance**—Be sure you use your correct street address and zip code. Include terms to help the person searching, such as the name of your neighborhood, suburb, and distinctive landmarks.

- **Prominence**—Google searches for reviews, articles, links to your page, blogs, and more. Be sure you are present on the social Web. Using Google's suite of online tools like Google+ and Google+ Local is a key way to accomplish this.

You do not need to have a Google+ page in addition to your Google+ Local listing. I recommend that you consider creating a page, however, because it gives you a space to interact and share with your customers. When you set up your Google+ page, choose "Local Business or Place" to get started.

Get creative with the content that you share from your page. You can share employees of the month, more information about your owners, photos, and videos from your business. Share more information about the history of your business: Does the building itself have a story worth sharing? If you own a restaurant, consider a Hangout On Air with your restaurant's chef preparing the daily special. This could make for a fun way to engage your customers and tempt them to pay you a visit tonight. Use the About section to also tell your visitors more about your business.

Your network of customers and potential customers are searching for a business like yours right now. Will they find you?

Give Google+ a Try

I made this chapter brief enough for you to get a grasp of Google+ to decide if it will work for you. Remember to consider who you are trying to reach first. Use your personal profile to network using circles and communities. Consider creating a community for your industry to grow your personal or business network. Take some time to try a hangout to interact with your peers or customers.

If you have a business, you may want to consider creating a Google+ page. Use hangouts on Air to interact with your customers on your page. Consider relevance, distance, and prominence when providing your Google+ Local information.

Determine if your peers, potential employers, or customers are users before investing too much of your time. Google+ will likely continue to evolve, but I don't expect it to disappear altogether. Remember that Google is an online powerhouse that is heavily invested in the success of its products.

Endnotes

1. http://socialfresh.com/seriously-who-is-using-google-plus-and-why/

2. www.flowtown.com/blog/whos-using-google?display=wide

3. www.mediapost.com/publications/article/163492/youtube-the-monster-search-engine-you-cant-ignor.html#axzz2FK7A2MH1

4. www.google.com/+/learnmore/hangouts/onair.html

5. http://googleblog.blogspot.com/2012/12/google-communities-and-photos.html

6. https://plus.google.com/u/0/communities/109526871298488380216

8

Content Is the Glue
That Binds Us Together

Think back to your best friends from childhood. You connected with your closest friends over shared interests. For me it was Legos, Star Wars, ninjas, Dungeons and Dragons, and computers. As I got older it was music, film, and technology. Then it became travel, entertainment, social media, and marketing.

What shared interests did you have with your friends? What brought you together? Content is the glue that binds us together. The content can be an album or music from a band, a game you play together, or a television show you enjoy.

Today the Internet is host to much of the content consumed. Videos are on YouTube, music is on Spotify, and photos are on Flickr and Instagram. Most forms of great content can be found online, so it's little wonder that people spend so much time there. To make strong online relationships, you must find similarities with the people you connect with. Content is the secret sauce.

The content you create can range from photos and videos to blog posts and tweets. It's this content that gives your networks a taste of who you actually are. The photos you share of your kids, pets, and coworkers all show a more intimate and human side, while 140-character tweets share insight, opinion, and humor.

You share the content you create with links on your splash pages or with posts on your blogs. Bloggers use their photos, videos, podcasts, ebooks, and whitepapers to drive traffic to their sites. The content is then shared with the world, and additional sharing is encouraged through social sharing buttons on each blog post.

In this chapter, I write about how new content creation tools and services connect and grow networks through the content you produce. Your professional networks grow when you resonate with people who you have things in common with. Businesses use this content to humanize their companies by giving a sneak peak at who, what, and where they are.

Rolling and Shooting: Content Through Video and Photography

According to Pew Research Center's Internet & American Life Project, "Forty-six percent of Internet users post original photos and videos online that they have created themselves, and 41% curate photos and videos they find elsewhere on the Internet and post on image-sharing sites."[1]

A study in the United Kingdom revealed a 40% increase in the average number of photos taken among camera phone owners from 2009 to 2011.[2] All indications are pointing at the collective move to what is being called the *Visual Web*.

People point, shoot, and share countless videos and photos every day. As I mentioned previously, this content gives others a taste of who they are and what their interests are. Not only can the photographs and videos be used for you to share, they can also be used to learn more about the creators who may be (or may become) part of your network.

In Chapter 1, "Do Your Homework," I wrote about how to do your homework and research people and companies before going on a job interview or sales call. If the sales lead or human resource manager you are meeting is online (and the chances are increasing that he is), you may be able to find commonalities by reviewing the person's photographs and videos on his social profiles. I recommend commenting on a fun video or photograph he shared if you have already met in person, but remember not to come off too eager by commenting on all of his content. You don't want to scare him off.

If you're a student, you should take and share photos from guest lectures, outings, or workshops. Give snooping recruiters and human resource professionals an idea of your life and why you would be an ideal candidate. Depending on the job you're seeking, videos and photographs can certainly help to sell yourself as a creative professional.

If you're hosting a meetup or conference, be sure to take plenty of photos and share them on the event's Facebook page or your company Flickr account. Attendees will visit your photos to relive the event and see if they were photographed. Encourage photo album visitors to tag one another so everyone can see the names of the people they were speaking with during the event. This helps greatly at reconnecting people post-event and continuing the conversation.

As an attendee, be sure to tag your photos from events you attend with the event name and corresponding hashtag. Share your best photographs by posting them to the event's Facebook page. This would be an ideal time to interact with your network by asking what everyone thought of the event or a specific speaker.

Whether you're representing yourself or a business, your photos and video humanize your brand. Photos tell a story and can express your personal side that not everyone sees. I feel more connected to the people I follow on Facebook, Instagram, and Flickr when I see snapshots and snippets of their daily lives. When I return home from a conference, I often connect with the people I enjoyed meeting. Once connected, I can learn more about them from their photos. I may learn that they also have young kids, that they recently vacationed in one of my favorite destinations, or perhaps that they enjoy the same beverages as I do (Guinness or coffee, in case you're wondering).

Instagram

Launched in October 2010, Instagram has quickly become one of the leading photography sharing social networks, growing astronomically since its debut. I have been using Instagram since November 2010, and I instantly fell in love with it because of the quick interactions you receive from followers. I also enjoy seeing more intimate photos of life outside of the 9-to-5 for my friends, colleagues, and companies.

Instagram is a photography app for iOS and Android smart phones that lets you use creative filters to change the appearance of your images. The filters are certainly what draw people into using the app, but the interactions are what keep people coming back. In just a simple gesture of tapping the screen twice, you can add a heart to the image representing that you like it. You can also leave a comment and reply to other comments.

Instagram made big waves in April 2012, when Facebook announced it had acquired the company for one billion dollars.[3] At the time of this writing, Instagram has 90 million monthly active users, and 40 million photos are added per day.[4]

How Do You Network on Instagram?

You can learn a lot from someone you're following on Twitter over time, but by following them on Instagram, you learn instantly. As a father of two young children, I love seeing photos of my network's children. I've learned that Bob has two young girls my kids' age, Chris loves to ski, Sheila is vacationing in Toronto, Mary spends much of her time in lecture halls studying finance, Avery lives in a cabin by the lake, George loves hiking, Jen is a foodie...you get the idea. By taking the time to flip through, like, and comment on the photos from your connections, you interact at a much more personal level. Photography is art, and those sharing photos reveal a more honest self that may not be expressed as easily on other social networks.

Use Instagram to share photos of your life, too. Try to share quality photographs, but understand that these are not necessarily going on exhibit anywhere. The point of sharing photos is to give people a view of what you're all about. Share photos of whatever you're comfortable with. Ideas include your children, food you've prepared, travel destinations, workplace, friends, conferences, outdoor locations, your office, or your home.

Each day Instagram photos receive 8,500 likes and 1,000 comments per second.[5] Never ignore your commenters and those who have liked your photographs. Be sure to reply to people who take the time to leave you a comment, even if it's just to say, "Thanks." Take additional steps to check out those who have liked and left comments on your photos. Instagram works the same way Twitter does, so you can easily follow a new person of interest.

Do a search for things you enjoy. At the time of this writing, I just completed an intense session of the Monopoly board game with my kids. I ran a search for "Monopoly" in Instagram and was amused by the array of photos that appeared. I like to review search results of companies I enjoy, clients (who I always enjoy), products I like, and places I have lived, like Galway, Ireland; Edinburgh, Scotland; Prague, Czech Republic; Toronto, Canada; and Nashville, USA. Follow the photographers who you enjoy.

Consider sharing your own photos on Facebook, Twitter, Google+, and Flickr. Instead of just automatically publishing the photo, include a question like "Guess what this is?" or "Who recognizes this city skyline?" Challenge your followers to add the best caption to a photo; the results are often hilarious.

Don't just follow the photographers who you enjoy. Take some time to like, share, and leave comments on their photos. Instagram also has a search function within the app, so you can search for things like a conference hashtag or a product name. You can also use a third-party browser-based service like Tripnity's excellent Statigr.am, which also provides you with statistics and allows you to like and comment on photos right from your computer. If you work with a large brand, a quick search may reveal photos of your products photographed by your customers. What a perfect opportunity to introduce yourself!

Set up an account, and let me know when you do. I would love to see your photos. You can find me at instagram.com/davedelaney.

Flickr

Flickr is Yahoo!'s popular photo sharing service. It was launched in February 2004, and has long been one of the most popular photo sites. Born six years before Instagram, Flickr has a long-standing reputation of providing a great service to novice and professional photographers.

You can perform searches for photos you're interested in or flip through your contact's photographs. You can easily find your contacts by connecting your Flickr account with your email or Facebook account. As you connect with your network, be sure to leave comments and favorite the best photos you come across, both by your contacts and from strangers.

 Tip

Using the Instagram application? Did you know you can post your photos directly to your Flickr account?

Flickr has user-created groups that you can join and contribute to. These groups are an excellent way to meet like-minded photographers online. There are more than 10 million groups on Flickr,[6] everything from Back The Blue,[7] a group for law enforcement professionals who share photos of police vehicles, to Art Photography,[8] a group for artistic photographers to meet and share stunning artistic photos. Each group's members interact with one another by leaving comments and selecting photos as favorites (similar to clicking Like on other social platforms). My guess is that you'll find a group that meets your interests. If not, consider starting your own. Don't simply join and post photos, though. Interact with the other photographers by leaving comments, asking questions, and selecting your favorites.

Use Sets to pool your photos from an event or location. Think of these public or private sets as photo albums. Be sure to tag your friends, colleagues, and customers in the photos they appear in. Assuming your friend is a Flickr user, she will be alerted when she is tagged. You can also choose Share the Image Directly using the Share button on the photos you admire.

The more comments you leave, the more comments you'll receive over time. Use Flickr to show the human side of your business or the behind-the-scenes of your life. Chris Wage is the chief operating officer of a Nashville-based interactive agency, but he uses Flickr as an outlet to showcase the people and city of Nashville through his stunning photography. (See www.flickr.com/photos/cwage/.) Chris Suspect is the manager of public outreach for a company in Washington, D.C. Suspect's photos capture the eclectic array of everyday people he sees and meets. Many of his photos are conversation starters and give a rare glimpse into the lives of Americans. (See www.flickr.com/photos/csuspect/.) As an example of an amazing Flickr account for a business, have a peak at photos from The White House (yes, *that* White House) at www.flickr.com/photos/whitehouse.

What I love about photography is it gives a different perspective to who you are. For example, a popular author may not write about her family or hobbies, but a look at her Instagram or Flickr profile reveals pictures of her personal life outside of writing.

Deciding between Instagram and Flickr can be a tricky one. Personally, I prefer to use both. I have been a Flickr user for years now, so I can share and back up my photos. I can instantly access my Flickr account from its impressive app on my iPad to share private photos with my family. Instagram is a more public collection of artistic photos I shoot. When I take a photo using Instagram, I always post it to my Flickr account, too. This way I have the photo backed up elsewhere online.

Avoid oversharing your photos across every social network. Instead, choose a few favorites to share from time to time. Avoid sharing more than one or two in a day.

Creative Commons

A rich and interesting photograph is the perfect complement to a blog post, but you may not always have the best personal photo for the occasion. If you need to find original photography for your blog post, presentation, or other digital work, I recommend searching Flickr's Creative Commons section: flickr.com/creativecommons.

Creative Commons is an open license alternative to copyrights that gives artists the choice to select how they want their work to be used. For example, a photographer may choose a noncommercial Creative Commons license, which means

you must only use it in noncommercial work. Perhaps they choose an Attribution-ShareAlike license, which means anyone can take their work and remix it for commercial or noncommerical work. Wikipedia uses this license.

Visit CreativeCommons.org to learn more and to find great content that you may use following the original artist's wishes. Consider licensing your own work with Creative Commons, too.

YouTube

YouTube is no small potato! In 2010, the hot video sharing site was named as the second most popular search engine[9] (after Google), and it's still believed to hold the position. Like the name of this chapter suggests, content binds people together and gives them a reason to connect.

YouTube is the perfect platform for you to promote yourself and grow your network by sharing thoughtful videos that inform, entertain, or inspire your viewers. These videos can be either ones that you find and feel your network can benefit from, or they can be original videos you create specifically for your network.

When I consider YouTube, I automatically think of inspiring people who have used it to make their careers take off—people like Justine Ezarik, known best as iJustine.

In August 2007, Justine received a 300-page, double-sided bill from AT&T Mobility for her iPhone data usage, which was mailed to her in a box. The result was a one-minute video[10] she uploaded to YouTube that has received more than 3 million views to date. In the video, Justine unpacks her ridiculously long phone bill (http://www.youtube.com/watch?v=UdULhkh6yeA).

Justine used her Internet fame gained from the video and her other online video work to grow her network. She continues to produce, star, and guest star in web videos and television programs. The point, though, is that she also continues to interact with her fans, which is something she has done throughout her career.

I assume that had she simply produced the one video and went on with her life, she would not be as successful as she is today. From producing great content and interacting with her friends and fans, she has accumulated more than 1.3 million subscribers to her main iJustine YouTube channel.[11]

Not Everyone Can Be a YouTube Celebrity

Not everyone can be a YouTube celebrity like iJustine. She has taken her role as an actor, comedian, and web video producer and has successfully made it her

full-time job. You may be asking, "Dave, how can *I* use YouTube to grow my network?" You *are* asking this, right? Right?

Everybody is an expert in something. If you're a student about to graduate, you already have expertise in the area you studied. Sure, you may not have put it into professional practice quite yet, but the knowledge you have gained is enough to share with those who want to learn from you.

If you're an education student, why not create videos that will help fellow educators or future students? Take a moment to jot down some lesson activities you have learned or created during the past few years of study. Pretend that someone just asked you the question. Pose in front of your webcam or phone camera and answer the question. Upload the video to YouTube and share it across your social channels. Are you a member of your school's LinkedIn or Facebook group? Post your videos there to share with your classmates and professors. Done. Easy.

iJustine's AT&T bill video is short, which is a good thing. (We have short attention spans.) The background noise makes the video appear more amateur than professional, but this doesn't matter. In some cases, the video will appear more authentic by not being overly produced. Don't worry about the quality as much as the content itself.

If you're not a student but a professional seeking to grow your network, why not create a video series on the area of your specialty? Promote the videos across your social accounts like Facebook, LinkedIn, Twitter, and Google+, and be sure to answer the questions you receive in the comments on YouTube.

ZeFrank[12] is one of my favorite YouTube personalities. In many of his inspirational videos, he answers questions that his fans submit. His videos are entertaining, uplifting, and often funny. He builds a strong bond by sharing his network's videos and music. Another example is Blendtec's famous "Will It Blend"[13] series, which features Tom Dickson attempting to blend viewer-submitted suggested items like an iPad and other unimaginable things in a blender. This series started as a single video idea on YouTube, but after it's sudden success, Blendtec knew they had a hit video series on their hands. Check out "A Show with Ze Frank" at youtube.com/zefrank1 and "Will It Blend" at youtube.com/blendtec.

Be present and engage with the people who share and interact with your videos. This is how to grow relationships and broaden your networks. Pay attention and respond to the positive comments people leave. Remember my tip from Chapter 3, "Your Home on the Web Needs More Than a Welcome Mat," about not feeding the trolls. YouTube gets its fair share of bullies who leave hurtful comments. Ignore them and move on.

YouTube for Business

If you own a business or you want to create a YouTube channel for your business, spend some time thinking about the content you want to create. What types of videos will help your customers and potential customers?

A great idea is to refer to your customer support team for the questions and issues your customers have most frequently. Compile a list of 10 or 20 of these questions, and begin a series of videos answering each question. Soon you'll have plenty of great videos to share with the world.

Encourage viewers to leave comments, and be sure to answer them. Embed the videos on your blog or company site so your visitors can find them. Promote them across your social profiles.

If you've built a decent following on one (or all) of your social channels, why not ask your customers, friends, and fans to submit their questions? Then pick the best ones to produce additional videos.

Videos are one of the best ways to humanize a brand. Remember that customers, employers, and future employees all prefer to see the actual people behind the brands. We naturally seek connections with humans more than logos, so consider this when you are creating your videos.

McDonalds Canada "Our Food. Your Questions."

A good example of a brand using YouTube effectively is McDonald's Canada.[14] In May 2012, the company launched a YouTube series called "Our Food. Your Questions." Each video features senior staff answering questions received from the public. For example, executive chef, Dan Coudreaut, answers, "What is in the sauce that is in the Big Mac?"[15] The video has been viewed more than 2 million times. Over 50,000 people have viewed Jeff Kroll, senior VP of supply chains, explain where McDonald's Canada gets its hamburger patties from.[16]

Consider how your company can answer your most common questions in a short video series on YouTube. As I mentioned before, be sure to answer the comments you receive from everywhere you share the videos.

Videos should always aim to inform and entertain. The McDonald's Canada videos are all well produced and appear high budget. You should not fret if you have a small budget. One of my favorite YouTube videos by a business was "Battle at F-Stop Ridge"[17] by The Camera Store.

In the video, several staff members attack one another in an epic photography battle with clear inspiration from such war film classics as *Saving Private Ryan*, *Platoon*, and *Full Metal Jacket*. The video is brilliantly made with the men shooting

cameras instead of guns, slow motion effects, and ear-bursting snaps and explosions of each camera's shutter and flash.

To date, the video has received nearly 2.5 million views. Not bad for a shoot that only took two days to film and edit. You can bet that business improved as a result of so many people suddenly learning about The Camera Store. In fact, director Jordan Drake went on to offer digital video classes at The Camera Store to its customers.[18]

Ian Greant, The Camera Store's director of new media, told me that from a branding and reputation basis, the video provided an incredible return on investment. He said that the business saw an increase in positive opinion from its customers and suppliers as well.

Be sure that your videos are entertaining or informative, and bonus points if you can achieve both. Imagine that your favorite local business created a viral video sensation. I bet you would do your best to find a reason to pay the business a visit.

Network with the People Around You: Foursquare

When you share your location across your social profiles, you're creating tiny pieces of content for your network around you. Although it's important to use online tools and services to connect and meet people to grow your network, it's key to meet them in real life (IRL), too. When you meet people in person, your relationships become solidified. Sharing your location and searching for your friends around you using Foursquare is a fine example of how you can use a service to connect in person.

Foursquare is a location-based service (LBS) for smart phones that allows you to "check in" to locations and connect with friends. Nearly 30 million people use the popular LBS, with more than 3 billion check-ins recorded every day.[19] By using Foursquare, you notify your network of your location. This works well when you're traveling, but it can be equally fun from your home city.

I met a friend once for an early dinner. The restaurant was located along a strip of popular bars and restaurants in Nashville. When my friend left for an appointment, I was left feeling the urge to stay out a while longer. I opened Foursquare on my iPhone and found several friends were at a pub just a few doors away. I promptly walked down and joined them.

When a person checks in to a business the most, he is awarded the title of Mayor via Foursquare. The mayor receives a virtual badge that Foursquare awards. This may sound silly but can become quite competitive. A business owner can check Foursquare to see who the mayor is and reward him with a special offer.

Foursquare began as a simple game where people who checked-in to specific locations or locations during a specific time would receive virtual badges for achieving this. For example, I was once on a friend's pontoon boat, and I decided to check-in. When I did this, I received the "I'm on a Boat!" badge named after the popular song at the time. If you have checked into ten different venues, you receive the "Adventurer Badge", or if you have been to the same place three times in one week, you receive the "Local Badge."

If you own or work for a business, consider joining the one million[20] other businesses now using the popular LBS. Visit business.foursquare.com to claim or add your business. You can then post updates with daily specials, employees of the month, or special events occurring. Foursquare also provides businesses with a free analytics dashboard to monitor the number of check-ins received and who the most frequent customers are. That is a perfect opportunity to reach out to say thank you and broaden your network.

If you're exhibiting at a conference, promote your booth on Foursquare. It only takes a moment to set up the location from foursquare.com. When you return home, you can visit the location online to see who checked in (visited). Write to each person to say thank you and invite them to connect with you elsewhere on the Web, like Facebook or Twitter. As an attendee, you may want to visit your profile later to review each booth or business where you checked in. You can leave a tip, comment, or like the business later.

Another key feature of Foursquare is tips. I use this frequently when I check in to businesses. For example, I may share my favorite menu item at a restaurant, a hotel tip about avoiding rooms above the pool, or an airport tip where there are ample power outlets for technology starving travelers. It's common courtesy to like the tip when you find it helpful, so the person who wrote it is notified that you found it useful. Consider leaving a comment or question on a tip you come across. If someone takes the time to write the tip, the least you can do is say thanks if you find it helpful.

As a business owner, I would carefully monitor my business on Foursquare so I could reply to compliments or concerns that my customers left. Building your network means connecting with your customers on a personal level. If they're kind enough to leave a tip, you should take a moment to respond with a reply or a like of your own. Show your customers that you're listening.

Claim your business on Foursquare at business.foursquare.com and then download the iPhone or Android app to see who your mayor is, interact with your customers, and more.

Location, Location, Location: Yelp

Yelp.com is a site and app that connects people with local businesses. If you own a brick and mortar business, you should search yelp.com to see if your business has already been added by your customers. The main purpose of Yelp is to allow your customers to leave reviews for future customers, so far over 36 million reviews[21] have been written.

Business owners or managers should take the time to set up a free account and claim their business. By claiming your business, you can share Yelp Deals, add photos of your business and staff, and most importantly you can reply to reviews your customers have left. This is a good way to build rapport by thanking them for positive feedback and for addressing negative feedback that you may have received.

Review the information about your business like address, phone number, and hours of operation to be sure it is correct. If your information is incorrect on your Yelp listing, you will unknowingly be losing business.

Pinterest

By now you've likely heard of Pinterest, the ridiculously popular social bookmarketing site. Pinterest is a site dedicated to sharing visual content. It has reached a unique U.S. audience of more than 27 million people already![22] You follow your friends and find new friends by exploring content using the site's search functionality. Each user has "boards" that they virtually "pin" visual content to that they find on the Web. Picture a traditional cork board in your office to help you understand the terminology.

If you have a clear understanding of who you're trying to connect with, you may choose Pinterest to engage your audience, especially if you want to connect with women. A study by the The Pew Internet & American Life Project found that 12% of online adults say they use Pinterest, which is dominated by women. Nearly a fifth of online women (19%) use Pinterest.[23]

Pinterest is now the third most popular social networking site behind Facebook and Twitter.[24] Using Pinterest to share eye-catching, visual content can drive a huge amount of traffic to your blog. In fact, in a report by Shareaholic, it was found that Pinterest drives more referral traffic than Google+, YouTube, and LinkedIn combined[25]!

If you run a business with an online presence, you are wise to consider making your content easy to share, or in this case "pin." You can do so by adding a Pinterest Pin button to your blog or by running contests encouraging your customers to pin items that link back to your site.

Users create multiple boards dedicated to specific categories, such as recipes, designs, infographics, logos, and so on. Anything on the Web that has a great visual is fair game for Pinterest. As I mentioned, it's better to make your content easily *pinnable* to encourage your visitors to share it.

Poor pinners pin only their own content. To reap the most benefit, use Pinterest to find your friends via email, Facebook, or Twitter. Then choose to follow the ones you are most interested in. Once you have done so, you can visit Pinterest.com to see your friends' latest pins and repin them to your own boards, like them, share them across the social web, or leave a comment. Leaving a comment is always the most time consuming but can also be the most rewarding because people always appreciate the extra personal touch.

By searching Pinterest for boards of items you're interested in, you can find new people to follow and connect with. These relationships can easily become closer as you interact with the users and get to know them better. For example, if you're a jewelry designer, you can use Pinterest to get inspiration, find and follow other designers, bounce creative ideas off one another, and share and promote others in your network.

Clare Hillerby[26] is a gifted jewelry designer in Manchester, UK. She originally set up a Pinterest account for research and inspiration. She told me that it's a wonderful way to see what people like. She explained that she has met many other jewelers, gallery owners, and curators through Pinterest. She uses old postcards and photographs in her jewelry, which makes it very personal. Using Pinterest, she is able to show people what she does and give them insight into her world, which she believes is an important part of her process.

Clare shared that she also uses Pinterest to learn more about galleries, because they often tend to pin the items they have on exhibit and for sale. She has found that galleries are often easier to contact via Pinterest than through their websites.

Pinterest may be the perfect icebreaker at a social event. When Clare met a fellow jeweler who she deeply admired, the first thing the woman said was, "I love your pins!" It was an instant conversation starter once the two met in person.

Pinterest for Business

Businesses seeking a spike in traffic to their sites and blogs should definitely consider making pinning their content as simple as possible. According to Comscore, "Pinterest is the fastest growing social media site in both unique visitors and clicks on search engines."[27] Comscore has also revealed that Pinterest users spend more money, more often, and on more items than any of the other top five social media sites."[28] Do you need any more convincing?

To get started, I recommend that you visit Business.Pinterest.com. The steps are simple for getting your business profile set up and verified. Use Pinterest to pin and share content you find online that you think your customers will appreciate. Be sure to use it to promote your own products, special offers, and contests too, but avoid over-promoting yourself. If you offer a service, pin infographics, charts, or any other visual content that clearly defines what your company does.

If your business makes a popular product, there's a good chance your customers have pinned it. A pin is as good as a like in the case of Pinterest. Visit Pinterest.com and search for your company or products by name and see what comes up. If someone takes the time to pin your product, it's likely because she enjoys it and wants to share it with her network.

Be sure to like and leave comments on your products that are being shared by your customers. Use the comments to ask them a question about their experience with the product. You can ask them what they like about it or how they would improve it. With enough feedback, perhaps a blog post is in order, taking care to mention those who pinned in the first place.

You may want to have your own meetup or Pin Up. Let's say you own or work for a bakery. You could invite your customers, friends, and fans to your Pin Up to make and decorate holiday cookies together. Encourage participants to take photos and pin them. Offer a discount to your store to the person whose cookie receives the most repins.

I've had conversations with people who aren't convinced Pinterest is for them. When the conversations reveal that they work as interior designers, architects, and event planners, I feel like shaking them by the shoulders to tell them why they should use Pinterest.

I tell interior designers to use Pinterest to pin photos of their best designs and to interact with other designers and fans of the art. Architects should use Pinterest to pin concepts to get feedback from followers. They should also use it to promote their portfolios and to connect with others in the industry. Event planners should have a board with photographs and sketches of their best work. By pinning your visual work, you can promote your business, give potential clients an overview of your style and capability, and grow your network by connecting with other industry professionals through liking, repining, and commenting on their work.

Don't forget to avoid only pinning photos of your products. Create boards for books, inspiration, infographics, great designs, recipes, architecture, and anything that you enjoy and you believe your followers will enjoy. Find your customers and interact with them. The social web is for socializing!

StumbleUpon

StumbleUpon is a social sharing site similar to Pinterest but in a less visual, organized way. Twenty-five million members[29] stumble once every three minutes while they're at work.[30]

StumbleUpon users set up an account and choose categories of interest. They then install the StumbleUpon browser bar, which gives them a Stumble button. A press of the button loads a random site that fits one of their categories of interest. Users use the Thumbs Up/Thumbs Down buttons to indicate whether they like or dislike the site that's revealed.

I've stumbled upon many interesting sites that I never would have found were it not for this service. When creating an account, StumbleUpon can scan your email address book and your social profiles to find friends who are already using the service. Once you're connected, you can begin to send sites of interest directly to others using StumbleUpon's simple interface. Sending an occasional site you find that will be of interest to a contact is a nice way of sparking a conversation or letting someone know you were thinking of him.

Both StumbleUpon and Pinterest are among the top sources of web traffic. This is important if you're trying to drive people to your blog. I don't recommend sharing all your blog posts on StumbleUpon, because it's not supposed to be used this way. Some of the best content I've found on StumbleUpon include items like photographs, videos, tutorials, comics, blog posts with lists, and infographics. Select posts you feel the community and your followers will enjoy the most. Share your own content occasionally, but focus more on sharing other people's content you find on the Web. Use the best content you stumble upon as inspiration for blog posts of your own. StumbleUpon is a treasure trove of compelling content!

Be sure that your site or blog has a StumbleUpon badge to make it dead simple for your visitors to follow you. Visit StumbleUpon.com/dt/badges/create. You should also make sure your social sharing plug-in includes StumbleUpon, so readers can easily share your blog posts.

Use StumbleUpon to discover the great content hidden on the Web. When you discover an interesting or entertaining blog post, video, image, or infographic, be sure to hit the Thumbs Up button in your browser and include a brief description if possible. If you like what you see on the rest of the author's site, consider subscribing to her blog and leaving comments to express how much you enjoyed it. Bloggers love comments and their content being shared.

SlideShare

SlideShare is a presentation sharing site originally developed for companies to share internal presentations and documents. Since being made available for public use, it has exploded in popularity as the best source for presentations on the Web.

Each month SlideShare receives 120 million visits and 3 billion page views.[31] Visitors browse for presentations on topics related to their industry. These topics range from education to venture capital/private equity.

When you create an account, you can connect it to Facebook to see who in your network is already using the service. You'll be surprised to see the number of people you know who are uploading their presentations and sharing other people's presentations.

As a student, you probably had to create presentations for your classes. Why not upload them and share them on SlideShare to gain exposure and meet people? Sharing this kind of content is a brilliant way to get yourself in front of potential employers and recruiters. Consider following the company accounts and individual accounts of people you're interested in learning more from.

If you don't have presentations, consider creating one. You can use Microsoft PowerPoint or Apple Keynote to easily build a presentation. Choose a topic that you feel your network would benefit from, and keep it visual and simple. I highly recommend Gar Reynold's *Presentation Zen* or Nancy Durate's *Resonate* as books to learn more about creating killer presentations. Take a few minutes to watch Nancy Durate's TED Talk "The Secret Structure of Great Talks."[32]

Once your presentation is uploaded on SlideShare, use your social channels to promote it. You can use the SlideShare app to embed the presentation on your Facebook page and the LinkedIn app to embed it on your LinkedIn profile. SlideShare makes it easy to embed presentations in your blog posts, too.

 Note

LinkedIn acquired SlideShare in May 2012.

In 2011, I created a presentation with tips for attendees of the South by Southwest festival in Austin, Texas. To date, the presentation has been downloaded (an option you can set on or off) nearly 240 times. I was pleasantly surprised to see it had been viewed more than 30,000 times.

Search SlideShare for presentations on topics you're interested in and you feel can benefit your network. Use your blog to embed the presentation in a post, and write your own commentary to give it context for your readers. You can also use

SlideShare to share videos, webinars called Zipcasts, and podcasts, which I will tell you more about in this chapter.

Slideshare for Business

SlideShare is a fantastic way to raise awareness of you and your brand. I mentioned how students can use it and how individuals can use it to gain knowledge about a particular topic and to provide content for their blog. Companies can also use SlideShare to share everything from conference presentations to annual reports.

Do a search on SlideShare to see if people have mentioned your company. Like their presentations and leave comments. Acknowledging feedback (positive and negative) is a good way to build loyalty and trust among your customers. Do this, and your professional network will grow naturally as a result.

Search for presentations that are related to your company based on your industry. Like those presentations, and share them on your company blog and social profiles. Don't stop at just leaving a comment or replying to comments. Click through each person to learn more about them and follow them on their own social profiles. Consider reaching out via that network. For example, if John Doe shares a great presentation you enjoyed, leave a comment and then share it on Twitter giving John a shout-out while you're at it.

Podcasting

My wife and I hosted a podcast from 2005 to 2008 about parenting. We were expecting our first child and decided to record some audio banter about what our experiences were like. The purpose was to create an audio baby book for the kids to listen to when they grew old enough to enjoy and probably be embarrassed by.

Podcasting was still in its infancy in 2005. We were inspired by other podcasts hosted by couples (or "couple casts")—shows like "The Dawn and Drew Show," "Zee and Zed," "The M-Show," and "The Catfish Show," to name just a few. Due to our parenting ignorance, we referred to ourselves as a couple of boobs. Our show was called "Two Boobs and a Baby" with the tagline "Follow the trials and tribulations of two boobs as they discover parenting one step/blunder at a time." We later added a plus symbol to the name when we added our fourth cast member, our daughter.

We learned a lot about creating a community from interacting with our listeners. For example, I created a forum so everyone could share their parenting tips and stories. It became a fun place to engage with our listeners, some of whom are still friends today.

There are two great ways to grow your network through podcasting. One way is to subscribe, listen, and interact with shows. The other is to create your own podcast and build a loyal listenership. I'll cover the easier one first.

Finding, Subscribing, and Interacting with Podcasts

The easiest way to find a podcast is to do a Google search for the topic of interest and the word *podcast*, for example: "gardening podcast" or "marketing podcast." Another good way is to search within Apple's iTunes in its podcast section.

All smart podcasters include a link to Subscribe in iTunes to their websites. From there you are just a click away from adding the podcast to your iTunes account. After you have subscribed, your MP3 player or smartphone should update with the most recent episode once it has been downloaded.

An alternative to using iTunes is to subscribe and update podcasts directly from your device. I recommend the Stitcher app from Sticher.com, Downcast app for iPhones and iPods from Downcastapp.com, and BeyondPod for Android from BeyondPod.com.

There are so many independent podcasts to choose from on just about every subject. Be sure to visit the supporting sites of the shows you enjoy most and interact with the host(s) and listeners by leaving a comment. Interacting helps you meet other fans of the show while encouraging the host. Visit your favorite podcast's Facebook pages and like them. You'll likely find a community of listeners there, too.

Use Twitter to interact with show hosts and promote your favorite podcasts. You can also visit the show page in iTunes and leave a high rating and comment for other potential listeners.

Podcasting is still heavily community driven, so think about other ways you can promote your favorite shows. It will help support the hosts and encourage them to keep pushing forward with new episodes rather than burning out and ending the show, which is known as *podfading*.

Listen to podcasts on topics you're most interested in. Try to mix up the shows you subscribe to from amateur to professional radio shows. Taking the time to tune into podcasts can be extremely beneficial. Why waste time with terrestrial radio in real time, when you can tune in to a show any time you like? I often refer to podcasting as "Internet radio on demand."

Podcasts can certainly entertain you, but they can also inspire and inform you by being thought provoking and educational. iTunes has an entire section called "iTunes U" (as in University) dedicated to sharing lectures from the best universities and colleges in the world. And it's all free!

Find the shows that meet your interests and subscribe. Leave comments and interact with the guest and hosts of the shows you enjoy. Like bloggers, podcasters produce content because they want to hear from you. They want to build relationships and grow their own networks just like you do.

I'm certain that winning your way to a podcaster's heart involves leaving comments and promoting their show via social networks. You will gain bonus points for leaving a rating and review under their listing in iTunes.

Creating Your Own Podcast

It's never been easier to start your own podcast. By creating a podcast, you can tell stories, provide opinion, do interviews, and entertain your listeners. I can't think of a more intimate form of content than an audio podcast, because your listener must focus on what you're saying to enjoy the show. They either turn up the volume in their homes, offices, or cars, or they plug in their headphones so they can only listen to you. Your voice is literally speaking, whispering, or shouting in their ears.

Although many people may jump on the podcasting bandwagon to try to find gold by "monetizing" their show, the true benefit is the relationships that are grown from the podcast. I have dear friends who I met either from communicating with one another online or meeting in person at conferences likes Podcasters Across Borders (PAB) and Podcast New Media Expo (PNME).

Creating a podcast today is much easier than ever before. I recommend that you do some deep thinking first, though, just as you would before launching a blog. Think about how your show will help your listeners and grow your network. Do a search in iTunes to find shows on similar topics and determine how your podcast will differ from the competition.

This chapter could be entirely dedicated to creating your own podcast. In fact, there are books about this very subject. Instead, I'll share a few tips to get started:

- Brainstorm topics.
- Know your audience.
- Find great guests if you have an interview show.
- Use a blog to host your podcast. You'll want to include a blog post to direct people when a new episode is available. Use the post to include your show notes, including information about your topic and links to items you mentioned.
- If you host an interview show, you can record the show using AudioHijack Pro (rogueamoeba.com/audiohijackpro) with Skype. Record the episode in AIFF format.

- Use Audacity (Audacity.SourceForge.net) to edit your show and export it as an MP3 file.
- Upload your MP3 to your server or use a service like libsyn (libsyn.com).
- Include a link to the MP3 in your corresponding blog post. Search for podcast plug-ins that are compatible with your blog software.
- Add your podcast to iTunes and Stitcher (Stitchr.com).
- You can also record your show using your smart phone with an app like SoundCloud (SoundCloud.com) or Audioboo (Audioboo.fm) to host your files. Just be sure to back up everything.
- Promote your podcast to your network. Invite them to be guests, and invite them to leave comments on your blog.
- You can learn more about creating a podcast from Apple at apple.com/itunes/podcasts/specs.html.

I recommend searching for communities dedicated to podcasting in Facebook groups, LinkedIn groups, and Google+ communities. Connect with fellow podcasters first, and grow your network by asking and answering questions.

I also recommend visiting PodcastAnswerMan.com and following Cliff Ravenscraft, who has turned his passion of podcasting into his profession. He shares plenty of great tips on his site dedicated to the topic.

Networking with Your Podcast

One of my favorite podcasts is "Six Pixels of Separation," a marketing show by author, journalist, and publicist Mitch Joel. Mitch has been podcasting steadily since 2006 and in that time has produced nearly 400 episodes. The show has evolved a bit over time, as yours will, too. Each episode is roughly 30 minutes and features interviews with top marketing professionals.

Mitch is a perfect example of a person networking effectively using podcasting. He does this by interviewing experts, which puts him on their radar and introduces him to industry leaders who he learns from during the interviews. The episodes are available for free to anyone, which means that listeners gain knowledge by tuning in. Listeners like me promote Mitch and his show, because I'm so thankful for everything I've learned over the years.

Mitch has always used "Six Pixels of Separation" to "softly" promote his digital marketing agency, Twist Image. He always mentions the agency, but he never goes in to overly promoting it or its services. Instead, he relies on interested listeners to visit the site to learn more about the agency's services.

Through years of great work and public speaking, Mitch has been dubbed "the Rock Star of Digital Marketing" by *Marketing Magazine,* and he has shared stages with Bill Clinton, Sir Richard Branson, and Malcolm Gladwell. From hosting hundreds of interviews on his podcast, you can bet that Mitch has grown his network tenfold, resulting in landing prime speaking engagements, new clients, and a strong professional network of friends and fans of his work.

Here are some key points to take away using "Six Pixels of Separation" as an example:

- Come up with an interesting concept. Mitch had one of the first shows dedicated to marketing.

- Distinguish yourself from the competition. Search other podcasts in your industry. How will yours be different? Tune in and decide how you will stand out.

- Don't be afraid to pivot your show's format. Mitch started his show only sharing his thoughts on industry-related topics. Over time, he began conducting interviews. Today the show is purely interview format. Go with what feels natural and works.

- Make the podcast easily accessible. Use links on your site, social sharing options on the blog, and add your show to iTunes and Stitcher.

- Network with other professionals and tell them about your show. Consider adding a link to your business card.

- Use your podcast to softly promote your company, but never be overly self-promotional.

- Educate yourself and your listeners. You can bet Mitch learns something new with every interview he conducts. By sharing his show, he shares the wisdom of his guests and his own with his listeners.

I've always admired Mitch because of his amazing podcast and blog, where he pontificates regularly about the marketing industry. You can tune in and read his posts at www.twistimage.com.

Content Is the Glue

When you get right down to it, content encapsulates everything you create online. Content can be as grand as an ebook or whitepaper or as brief as a tweet. The point is to create something that others will find useful. Make content that is informational or entertaining, and you get bonus points if you accomplish both at the same time.

I've only scratched the surface in exploring content and additional networks where you share what you find and create. Take notice and pay attention to your earliest

fans of your work. Support and promote them. They may stick with you through your entire career, and they may even become close friends.

Always consider who you're creating the content for, who you're sharing content with, and what you're trying to accomplish in doing so. Use it to promote yourself, but never be overly self-promotional. Instead, subtly use your original content to drive traffic back to your blog or website and encourage comments and interactions. Also, engage in conversations about the content you discover and share.

By creating and sharing compelling content, you promote yourself and ultimately grow your network from connecting with people interested in what you're sharing. Take note, though; this goes both ways. When you discover content you enjoy, be sure to take the time to learn more about the creator. She is sharing her photos, videos, tweets, and blog posts because she wants to hear from you and grow her own networks. It's the content that's consumed, shared, and created that binds people together.

Endnotes

1. http://pewinternet.org/~/media//Files/Reports/2012/PIP_OnlineLifeinPictures.pdf

2. http://blog.infotrends.com/?p=6913#more-6913

3. http://abcnews.go.com/blogs/technology/2012/04/facebook-buys-instagram-for-1-billion/

4. http://instagram.com/press/

5. http://instagram.com/press/

6. www.flickr.com/tour/?f=hp#section=watch-the-world

7. www.flickr.com/groups/backtheblue/

8. www.flickr.com/groups/art-photography/

9. www.siliconrepublic.com/news/article/16234/new-media/youtube-hits-2-billion-views-per-day

10. www.youtube.com/watch?v=UdULhkh6yeA

11. www.youtube.com/ijustine

12. www.youtube.com/zefrank1

13. www.youtube.com/blendtec

14. www.youtube.com/McDonaldsCanada

15. www.youtube.com/watch?v=rcu4Bj3xEyI&list=PLB8F066AFA8915464

16. www.youtube.com/watch?v=hDQYSi5giM8&list=PLB8F066
    AFA8915464

17. www.youtube.com/watch?feature=player_
    embedded&v=awq90APEVgw

18. www.thecamerastore.com/blog/2011/05/20/battle-f-stop-ridge-goes-
    viral

19. https://foursquare.com/about/

20. http://business.foursquare.com/

21. www.yelp.com/about

22. www.business2community.com/pinterest/nielsen-report-shows-
    explosive-pinterest-growth-0370178#0LA7HZLW2OD5xc2J.99

23. http://pewinternet.org/~/media//Files/Reports/2012/PIP_
    OnlineLifeinPictures.pdf

24. http://go.experian.com/forms/experian-digital-marketer-2012?WT.
    srch=PR_EMS_DigitalMarketer2012_040412_Download?send=yes

25. http://blog.shareaholic.com/2012/01/pinterest-referral-traffic/

26. www.clarehillerby.co.uk

27. www.comscore.com/Insights/Presentations_and_Whitepapers/2012/
    State_of_US_Internet_in_Q1_2012

28. www.comscore.com/Insights/Presentations_and_Whitepapers/2012/
    State_of_US_Internet_in_Q1_2012

29. www.stumbleupon.com/blog/stumble-through-2012/

30. www.stumbleupon.com/blog/stats/stumbleupon-stats-stumbling-
    during-the-day/

31. www.linkedin.com/company/slideshare

32. www.ted.com/talks/nancy_duarte_the_secret_structure_of_great_talks.
    html

9

If You Build It, They Will Come: Organizing Events

My journey of moving to a new town not knowing a soul has been an illuminating one. I firmly believe that were it not for the conferences and events I've helped build and create, I wouldn't be as well connected in Nashville (and beyond) as I am today. In this chapter, I share the lessons and tips I've learned through my experiences from organizing events.

If you feel overwhelmed a little, don't panic. Keep reading. Not everyone needs to build an event for hundreds of people and thousands of dollars. I'll tell you about some smaller events I've put together with little to no budget, which I hope will leave you inspired to start your own or get involved as a volunteer with other local events.

There's nothing better than meeting people in real life (IRL). You can use the social networks I've explained in the previous chapters to meet and stay connected to people and grow your networks, but it's the handshakes, hugs, and high-fives that truly bring people together.

In Chapter 1, "Do Your Homework," I explained how to find events and conferences you should consider attending. To super-charge your networking efforts, organize your own or volunteer to help others create an event.

Organizing BarCamp Nashville

On August 18, 2007, the first BarCamp Nashville conference (or *unconference*) was held to great success. The event was a jam-packed, 12-hour day, filled with speakers presenting their ideas on technology-related topics to hundreds of people. All of it was free. BarCamp Nashville was an important event for Nashville's emerging technology community, because it brought people together and shined a light on the city's technology scene.

The first BarCamp was held in Palo Alto, California in 2005. BarCamp was created as a free and open alternative to an invitation-only conference occurring at the same time. Attendees are encouraged to share their own presentations. It truly is a community event by the community, for the community. BarCamps have been held in hundreds of other cities across the world since that first one. The great thing about BarCamp is that it's relatively simple to organize your own. You can find the community wiki page at BarCamp.org for details on how to do so.

In this chapter, I share what I've learned from organizing events both locally in Nashville and in different cities. I hope this chapter leaves you inspired to connect with like-minded people to create your own small or huge event or volunteer to help in other's events for your community. The results are incredibly rewarding.

During the spring of 2007 when I moved to Nashville, I met Marcus Whitney, CTO at Emma, a popular email marketing company. Our meeting had been set up by Clint Smith, cofounder of Emma. Marcus was feeling me out for a position with the company, but before we had a chance to discuss this, we decided that Nashville needed a BarCamp. It was during that coffee that we began to concoct a plan.

I used Meetup.com to organize the first BarCamp Nashville "Crew" meetup. The purpose was to invite members of Nashville's technology community to meet to explore initial ideas about how the first BarCamp in the city would take shape. Those who attended made new friends that day. Some of them already knew each other, whereas others were meeting for the first time. For me, the new kid in town, everyone was a new friend.

A few people from Griffin Technology were present at the meeting. Griffin would be our second confirmed sponsor of the event next to Emma, which became my employer. I point this out because of the value of networking from organizing events. Just a few years later, I would be hired by Griffin Technology. Had I not helped organize the event, I don't know whether I would have ever met the guys at Griffin.

My cofounders, Marcus Whitney and Kelly Stewart, along with a team of dedicated volunteers, worked countless hours preparing for what would become an important annual technology event in Nashville. Organizing an event is a lot of work. Initial considerations are important.

It's essential that you work with a great team of people to help you create a valuable, memorable, and successful conference. Because BarCamp Nashville is a free event, it heavily depends on the support of the volunteers who come together to plan and execute it.

I mentioned that I created a Meetup group to invite anyone in the community to attend to help us. You won't need an army to help you. All you need is a small group of dedicated people.

Begin by asking your friends, family, and colleagues to help. Use Facebook, Twitter, Google+, and LinkedIn to get the word out and recruit volunteers. Consider contacting local colleges and universities to encourage student and faculty participation.

Ask anyone who has helped organize a conference, and they'll tell you that the best part is meeting like-minded people who end up becoming close friends, colleagues, business partners, cofounders, customers, and employees. Not only do you finish the event with an incredible feeling of satisfaction and knowledge, but you are left with a strong network of close relationships.

Encourage volunteers to write recommendations for one another on LinkedIn after the event has wrapped up. Volunteering gives many people their first taste of organizing events, especially in each person's area of responsibility. For example, the sponsorship manager should write a recommendation for the event coordinator, and the production manager should write a recommendation for the marketing manager. As volunteers, you are in this together, so be sure to pay compliments where compliments are due.

Your Event Site

There's plenty to consider in your site design, like style and content. I highly recommend that you create your site using a blogging platform such as WordPress. Review my suggestions in Chapter 3, "Your Home on the Web Needs More Than a Welcome Mat," when deciding how best to do this.

Ask your volunteers if they are or can recommend a good web designer. Perhaps you can exchange an in-kind sponsorship for their services if you can't find a volunteer to help you.

Use an editorial calendar to plan the blog posts you will write to pre-promote your event and to support your sponsors.

The following are some blog topic ideas:

- What is your event? Why did you create it?
- Who is organizing it?
- How do people register?
- Why should you be a sponsor?
- When and where will the event be held? (Make this very clear.)
- What were your experiences in planning it?
- What are related topics to the industry you are creating the event for?
- Do you have photographs and videos after the event?
- Are there guest posts from attendees who want to share their experiences afterward?
- Who are your sponsors? Thank them.

Event Size

What we loved about BarCamp is the free-form style and how it encourages everyone to participate. There are small BarCamps that are barebones, while others are larger events. Because the goal for BarCamp Nashville was to put Nashville on the "digital map" so the world would take notice of the great local technology companies and talent, we aimed to go as big as possible.

Whatever your event may be, you need to decide the scope. Are you trying to reach as many people as possible, or are you holding an event for a more intimate, select group of people? You need to have a clear vision of the event you envision before scouting locations.

Determining Budget

It's always safest to overestimate the budget needed to run an event. Consider important items such as venue rental; audio video equipment for presenters; swag such as tee-shirts, pens, bags; coffee and snacks; prizes; insurance; web hosting for your event website (blog); and advertising if you choose to place ads to promote the event.

Soliciting Sponsors

Brainstorm who your event will most benefit in the community. In the case of BarCamp Nashville, technology companies understood that by supporting the community, they would be promoting their company and its products and services.

Not only are there possible sales-related benefits, but there are potential employee recruiting possibilities, too.

Create a wish list of companies you think should sponsor your event. Use LinkedIn to see how (or if) you and your fellow organizers are connected. A strong LinkedIn network is beneficial for such a purpose. Compose a personal email to your potential sponsors to solicit their support. Don't spam your contacts by emailing everyone in one bulk message. Take the time to personalize your email and explain why you think their company would make a great sponsor.

Local companies likely have the best reasons to sponsor your event. However, don't only stick to your city limits. Consider large brands that may be appropriate. They often have bigger budgets for such sponsorships.

Showing Value to Sponsors

In the case of BarCamp Nashville, we were lucky to have local companies immediately take notice and offer to assist us as sponsors. However, we still had to create sponsorship packages and actively seek out additional funding.

Create a sponsorship document that breaks down several levels of sponsorship. BarCamp Nashville uses Worthy, Heroic, Legendary, and Epic. Brainstorm the benefits included in each level and what price each should be. I recommend taking a look at other conferences for an idea of how these levels are laid out. You can find BarCamp Nashville at www.BarCampNashville.org.

Answer their question, "What is in it for me?" before you approach sponsors. They will want to know what they can expect from financially investing in your event. Be sure you have the sponsorship document ready to send them, so you can email it when you hang up the phone. Once you have a soft commitment, send a formal agreement to make it official, and include the agreed sponsor level and price.

Remember that companies allocate budgets for event sponsorships many months in advance. The earlier you start exploring potential sponsors, the better the results will be.

Promoting Your Event

Use your event website as the main destination to direct people to learn more about the event. Ask your volunteer team to promote it to their networks, and you do the same. Write blog posts about your event on your personal or company blog. Encourage your team and sponsors to do the same.

One of the volunteers during the planning stage of the second BarCamp Nashville came up with an amazing idea to promote the event. The suggestion was to create

a "Blog Tour." A spreadsheet was created using Google Docs (now called Drive), which included headings like Date, Name, Blog Name, Blog Post Title, and Link to Blog Post. Volunteers, sponsors and members of the Nashville technology community joined the Blog Tour by writing a blog post about BarCamp Nashville. The spreadsheet worked as an editorial calendar, so everyone could see the dates that needed content and the topics of the posts ahead of time. There was one new blog post each day for the 30 days leading up to BarCamp Nashville. The posts were promoted across BarCamp Nashville's social profiles. Everyone who contributed was encouraged to share the other contributors' posts using Twitter, Facebook, Google+, and LinkedIn. Not only did this help spread the word, but it got everyone involved (and those reading the posts) excited about the event.

Create several web badges (small graphic banners) that include the name, date, and URL of the event. Create some for sponsors and speakers specifically, so they can include them on their sites or in blog posts on their own blogs. Request that they add a link back to your site, so visitors can click through to learn more. Be sure that the planning team members also use the badges on their personal sites and blogs.

Use LinkedIn to see who the planning committee knows at your local newspapers, alt-weeklies, and radio and television stations. Have a press release ready, and reach out to ask if they would be interested in learning about your event and why it's a news-worthy story. You may consider creating an in-kind sponsorship for a media company that can provide you with some free advertising.

Word of mouth is such an important part of a local community event. Be sure that everyone you know knows about it. Encourage others to tell the world, too. Consider using a ticketing service like Eventbrite.com. Not only will it make ticketing easier, it will include your event in its local listings, which helps to spread the word.

Print business cards or postcard-sized cards to have your team hand out to everyone they meet. You may even wrangle up a street team to hang posters and fliers at schools, bars, coffee shops, and local businesses.

Location Selection

Location, location, location! Your budget is obviously key when determining a good location for your event. Be sure that the location can accommodate factors like adequate power outlets (for laptops and mobile charging), free parking (if possible), enough room for a stage and your attendees, or enough rooms for multi-tracked presentations (occurring at the same time), central location that people can get to easily, and plenty of hall space or empty space for networking to take place.

Here are a few location ideas and considerations:

- **College or university**—Will you have the whole space or have to share it with other school functions?

- **Library meeting space**—Double-check hours and potential noise limitations.

- **Bar**—Will age requirements be a problem for some attendees?

- **Restaurant**—Will there be enough space to accommodate your attendee size?

- **Conference center**—Will there be too much space? Are there union rules to consider?

- **Religious institution**—Are there any restrictions in place you need to be aware of?

- **Hotel**—Will you need to use the hotel's catering and A/V services?

Organizing PodCamp Nashville

PodCamp is similar to BarCamp in many ways. In fact, it can be a little confusing. Like BarCamp, PodCamp is open and usually free to attend. It has multitrack presentations occurring concurrently like BarCamp does, and every attendee is encouraged to participate by presenting.

The first PodCamp was held in Boston, Massachusetts, in 2006, organized by Chris Brogan and Christopher S. Penn. Where BarCamp is more about technology, including hardware and software development, PodCamp is geared more toward online content such as podcasting (where the "pod" comes from in the name), blogging, self-publishing, and social media in general. You can learn more at PodCamp.org.

As a blogger and podcaster, I was excited by the opportunity to make our own PodCamp in Nashville. Together with Marcus and Kelly again, we organized our second free community event. We followed many of the same steps that we did for BarCamp, and on February 9, 2008, we held another successful unconference.

We were lucky, because our sponsors and many of the same volunteers returned to help us make PodCamp Nashville an incredible event. Take note here: The relationships that we made from the first event resulted in their return for our second event. Without successfully networking with the right people, PodCamp Nashville wouldn't have happened.

The combined content produced from BarCamp Nashville and PodCamp Nashville was massive. Countless news articles, blog posts, tweets, photographs, videos, and podcasts were produced to capture and share the news that a city best

known for its country music had much more going on in technology than many knew. There have been subsequent articles from outside of Tennessee about the technology scene in Nashville. I have no doubt that both events helped to achieve this, in part by producing the content and spreading the word, but also by connecting people who would later form technology companies of their own in Nashville.

I realize I've used two technology-focused events as examples, but there are alternative unconferences to choose from, such as REBarCamp for real estate professionals, WordCamp for WordPress developers, and ProductCamp for product managers and marketers. Do a search for other unconferences or "camps" in your industry. If one doesn't exist yet, consider creating your own.

What I love about organizing an unconference is that you're not doing it for profit. You're doing it to connect, grow, and support your community. That has always been my objective. I've made good friendships and had great business opportunities as a result of being involved with these events over the years.

Local Events and Mixers

In Chapter 1, I wrote about doing your homework and finding events to attend. In some cases, the event you are seeking does not exist—yet. With social networks and free event planning services, it is simple to create a new event. Create a Twitter tweet-up for your Twitter network. If your network is mainly on Facebook, use Facebook Events. You can also use free tools such as twtvite.com or meetup.com to set up your event or mixer. After you have your event invite ready, be sure to promote it across all of your social networks. The more attendees the merrier, right?

Geek Breakfast

After the initial buzz from the first BarCamp Nashville had died down, I felt a lull. I missed the energy from meeting so many amazing people all at once. We were already in the early phase of planning PodCamp Nashville, but I wanted a way to keep everyone together between the two events.

In December 2007, I created the first Geek Breakfast. The idea was simple. Find a great restaurant and invite anyone interested in Nashville's technology community to join us for networking over bacon, eggs, and coffee.

Geek Breakfast is unsponsored and unstructured. There are no guest speakers (no speakers at all). You end up meeting the people you sit next to and across from. Over the years, I have had small groups of about 10 people and large groups of up to 50 or 60.

One day an attendee from out of town said he wanted to create his own local Geek Breakfast. He asked me how to do it, and I jokingly responded that you invite geeks to breakfast. He pushed for a little more information, which resulted in GeekBreakfast.org being created by my friend and breakfast regular, Chris Ennis, and the team at CentreSource, a local interactive agency.

The site was set up so anyone could create a local Geek Breakfast easily. Soon the events started popping up across the United States in places like Chicago, New York, Silicon Valley, Tampa, Austin, South Carolina, Arkansas, and even countries like Canada, South Africa, and Australia.

I use Facebook events each month, so people can RSVP to attend. I do this in part to let the restaurant know approximately how many people to expect. I also use Facebook events because the invitation is always open and attendees can see who else is coming. An open registration can also help connect attendees after the event. For example, if I met someone but I didn't get her name, I can visit the event page on Facebook and put a name to the face. If you are creating an event that requires a ticket (free or paid), I highly recommend looking at Eventbrite. com. Eventbrite has the option for an open invitation. It works with Facebook, so attendees can see both their friends and others who are attending. Eventbrite also has a handy app you can use to check the status of your event from your phone. Other event-management tools include Anyvite.com and Pingg.com—both are fine services to help you manage your RSVPs.

Since 2007, Geek Breakfast has continued to connect local technology enthusiasts in each city. From time to time I hear stories of how people met at a Geek Breakfast, and it makes me happy to know it's worth the time it takes to facilitate our monthly meals. You can create your own or check to see if you have an existing local Geek Breakfast by visiting GeekBreakfast.org.

If technology is not your forte, create a monthly breakfast dedicated to the topic of your choice, and reach out to your network to invite people to join you. You'll never know unless you try.

Nashcocktail

Let's face it. Not everyone jumps out of bed bright-eyed and bushy-tailed and eager to speak coherent sentences in the morning. The only frequent issue I heard from some people about Geek Breakfast was it was too early for them to attend. Students had school and others had work conflicts that kept them from attending. They always asked for something later. I decided that Nashville needed a new networking event for social media fans, so Nashcocktail was born.

I invited BarCamp Nashville and PodCamp Nashville attendees on the Facebook pages and Geek Breakfast attendees from our email newsletter and Facebook page. Social Media Club Nashville helped to promote it too, and we had 50 people attend the first Nashcocktail.

Everyone spoke highly about Nashcocktail and encouraged me to continue to have monthly events. I also offer an inexpensive monthly sponsorship, so I have a little budget to buy prizes for attendees. I do several draws throughout the evening, saving the best one until last. Unlike Geek Breakfast, Nashcocktail is mainly standing room only. I like this format so attendees can walk around the room networking. You can learn more about it at Nashcocktail.com.

The following are some points you should review when organizing your own event:

- Does a similar event already exist? If so, how is your event different, and why should people come?
- Choose a venue that can accommodate your party's size. Does it have adequate parking?
- Is your event a cash bar/individual checks? Make this clear so attendees aren't disappointed.
- Graciously thank (and tip!) the servers. They can make or break your event.
- Take tons of photos, and share them on your Facebook page. Encourage fellow attendees to tag each other.
- Use Facebook events or Eventbrite to handle RSVPs. There are other options like Google+ events, Pingg.com, and Anyvite.com, but I prefer Facebook events and Eventbrite. Do your best to make the attendee list public so everyone can see who is attending.
- Introduce attendees to one another.
- Point out the new attendees, and ask your regulars to welcome them.
- Provide "Hello, My Name Is:" name tags to help ease attendees' introductions.
- Use sponsor money to buy prizes for giveaways, and save the best until the end of the event.
- Be sure to network and meet new people yourself.
- Use an email newsletter to keep attendees informed of future events.
- Use your favorite social networks to promote your event.

Doing Some Good

Networking is about helping others before helping yourself. The same applies to hosting or volunteering during an event. A good idea for the planning committee is to think of ways to give back to the community, like local charities, nonprofits, and specific local causes. Use your event to raise money and awareness, inspire volunteers, and bring a community together for a common cause. This can be done by donating a portion of your ticket sales, using your email or social channels to promote a cause, or informing attendees of a local need and ways they can help directly.

Two years ago, I saw an opportunity to bring my two monthly events together to assist our local food bank during the holiday season. I created a challenge between Geek Breakfast Nashville and Nashcocktail to see which group could collect the most food (Figure 9.1).

Figure 9.1   *The Geek Breakfast VS. Nashcocktail epic battle graphic, created by Kenneth White.*

I used each event's email newsletter, Facebook page, and Twitter to egg each group on and poke fun at one another. It was day versus night, AM versus PM, coffee-sippers versus booze-swillers. It was a good bit of fun to put both groups up against one another, especially since a number of attendees go to both events.

Together, we collected more than 500 pounds of food between our December events in 2011 and 2012. Consider how you can use your event to help your community, too.

In late 2009, a group of Twitter friends in Toronto were discussing the need to help the city's hungry. Together they reached out to their networks to create an annual party called HoHoTO.ca. It took the group just 20 days to organize the bash, which sold out in 9 days. More than 600 people attended the party, which raised $25,000 and collected a ton of food for the Daily Bread Food Bank. To date, the HoHoTO event participants and organizers have raised $225,000 and collected approximately 4 tons of food for the hungry[1]!

Organizing Meetups for Business Networking

Use meetups for your business to meet and connect with your customers, vendors, and anyone interested in attending. By taking the lead of organizing a meetup, you put yourself and your business at the head of the table. Attendees look to you to learn more about the topic of the meetup and for mutually beneficial introductions that occur during it. By providing a sound place for successful networking, you become the facilitator, which can result in new business, careers, and friends for those who attend. Also, this can come full circle and land you new business as well.

Events and conferences take a lot of time and energy to commit to, but the networking value is priceless. I wrote earlier about how I ended up getting hired by Griffin Technology as a result of working with them as a sponsor during the first BarCamp. I took my knowledge of organizing events with me when I was hired by Griffin to benefit the business.

At Gnomedex, a technology conference in Seattle, I organized a meetup for friends of Griffin. I used our email newsletter, Twitter, and Facebook page to invite Griffin customers in Seattle to join us for a pre-Gnomedex get-together at a local bar. Drinks and appetizers were on Griffin, as were the great products I brought along to give away to attendees.

I organized similar meetups in San Francisco before Mac World, a conference dedicated to Apple products; the South by Southwest (SXSW) festival in Austin, Texas; and the Consumer Electronics Show (CES) in Las Vegas. Why did I organize these events?

The point of organizing a meetup for your business is not to sell attendees anything, aside from the fact that your company is awesome. You want people leaving as new friends, not just customers. The next time they're in a store buying a product or shopping online, you hope they'll choose your product over others because of the relationship you've established. These new friends can also provide suggestions for future products and improvements on existing products, and they become advocates for your brand.

Networking with your customers and potential customers is key to building valuable relationships, which will result in revenue later. Consider sending them a thank-you email for attending your meetup. Include a link to a blog post you wrote about it and the photos you took at the event, and, if possible, add an exclusive coupon code to discount products on your site.

By humanizing your business or employer's business, you build real relationships. Networking with your customers can leave you with new product or service ideas, potential new employees, word-of-mouth advocates, and friends.

The next time you are attending a conference on your company's behalf, consider hosting a meetup. Who can you invite? Why not invite your customers in the city and not just the conference attendees? You can find them by creating a targeted Facebook advertisement, or you can email them from your own newsletter or database.

Serving as the Connector

There's no way for me to total the number of people I've met at the events I've helped organize. I always do my best to follow up with each person I meet by inviting them to connect on LinkedIn. In some cases, I email them to follow up on something we were discussing. When you get to know so many people, it's easy to become a connector.

When I see an opportunity for someone in my network, I rise to the occasion. As a connector, I frequently get asked whether I know candidates for employment positions or potential clients for businesses. This is that part when I remind you that networking is a two-way street.

Do your best to always be on the lookout for opportunities to help members of your network. For example, one member of my network asked if I knew any iOS developers. I introduced him to a contact I know who is a great developer, and the developer was hired. I helped two people by connecting them and asked for nothing in return. Nearly a year later, the person who was hired introduced me to someone who later became one of my clients. Connecting people works. Helping people to grow a network can be beneficial to everyone involved—even you. If you organize or volunteer at an event (and even if you don't), be sure to do your best to become a connector.

Organizing Paid Conferences

Organizing a large paid conference is no small feat. Although I've never done this myself, I turn to experts like Jason Keath, who runs the Social Fresh conference on social media marketing. Jason and I first met at a mixer held by the popular technology news site, Mashable.com, in Atlanta in 2009.

Take note here that it was because of Mashable's event that Jason and I met. The event was nothing overly complicated—just cocktails in a fun location. In an effort to connect with its readers, Mashable held mixers in several cities. I'll always be grateful, because I met so many people at these inexpensive events each summer.

When Jason and I met, we ended up discussing his ideas for conferences. He had several smart ideas, but Social Fresh stood out as a brilliant one. I continue to hear great feedback about Social Fresh from attendees and speakers each time he has a new event.

Jason began his career as an online marketing consultant. It was running his own conference that would shape his career, though. Jason has built much of his network from being a connector and taking the lead by creating Social Fresh.

In addition to running a successful conference, Jason turned to his website to begin to sell lessons and share great content related to social media marketing. He is now a full-time conference organizer and content producer. When I asked him what the number-one thing is he has learned about producing a conference, he replied "the value of partnerships."

It's the partnerships we strike with our event volunteers, sponsors, advertisers, attendees, and speakers that help us grow our professional networks.

Getting Started

Whether you decide to organize a small local get-together or a large paid conference, the most important ingredient is people. People will help you organize the event, they will help you find sponsors, they will become sponsors, they will be your presenters, and they will be your attendees.

By having a strong network of outstanding people, you can review and reflect on who can help make your vision for an amazing event a reality. Begin by asking yourself how a certain person's involvement in your event would benefit him. With that answer in mind, pick up the phone or write a short email to invite that person for a coffee to discuss the idea. It will only begin when you choose to start. And yes, if you build it they *will* come.

Endnote

1. http://hohoto.ca/about/

10

Listen Better.
Remember More.

The most basic of all human needs is to understand and be understood....The best way to understand people is to listen to them.
—Ralph G. Nichols

When you're meeting new people, you must be consciously listening. By listening to the stories and information you receive from new contacts, you create an instant connection. If someone realizes you're not listening, it leaves a negative impression that can be impossible to repair. By showing interest and responding appropriately as you listen, you gain the trust and respect of the other person.

I drive my wife nuts when she catches me not listening. It's amazing that she has stayed with me all these years. The truth is that we're both guilty of tuning each other out from time to time. You probably do this with your friends, family, or coworkers, too.

At the monthly social events I attend, I often take note of the conversations taking place around me. I watch as effective communicators listen affectionately to someone speaking. I also notice ineffective listeners as they gaze away from the person talking to scan the rest of the room or check their phones.

Stop reading this book for a moment. If you're in a public place, take a look at the people around you. Note how they're communicating with one another. Perhaps a couple at the table next to you is having a heated discussion about a recent news story. Maybe you see two business people sitting across from you at your gate in an airport speaking about the business trip they're about to embark on.

How are these people interacting with one another? Are they listening? One is probably doing the majority of the talking, while the other is either listening or chiming in periodically. Or perhaps the other person is simply *hearing* the gentleman and not actually *listening* at all.

At a recent social mixer I attended, I observed the attendees around me. One older woman was speaking to a much younger one. The younger woman kept looking up and over the shoulder of her peer instead of directly at her. She was probably scanning the room for people she knew or wanted to speak with.

Another man was speaking to a woman, or shall I say *at* a woman. His verbal assault was a nonstop banter about how he was fed up with his job. I noticed the woman smiling and nodding, probably doing her best to conceive an exit strategy.

Paul T. Rankin's "The Importance of Listening Ability"[1] reports that people spend 42% of their time listening, 32% talking, 15% reading, and 11% writing. With the majority of time spent listening and the most basic of human needs being to understand and be understood, it's important to take the time to develop effective listening skills so you can build strong, lasting relationships.

L.I.S.T.E.N.

I'll admit it. I've stopped listening when someone has been talking to me. I expect it has happened to you, too. What an awkward feeling it is when your colleague reaches the end of her monologue, and you're left unsure of what she has said. She stares at you questionably as you stare back with a blank look. You smile, nod, and do your best to appear as if you heard and understood every word. But in reality, her information went inside one ear and was whisked right out of the other.

In author Julian Treasure's 2011 TED Global presentation, "5 Ways to Listen Better,"[2] he explains, "We spend roughly sixty percent of our communication time listening, but we are not very good at it. We retain just twenty-five percent of what we hear."

By becoming a better listener, you learn to retain the information you hear, while reassuring and gaining trust from the one speaking. The best approach to this is to follow the *British Journal of Hospital Medicine*'s acronym L.I.S.T.E.N.[3]

L = Look interested; get interested

I = Involve yourself by responding

S = Stay on target

T = Test your understanding

E = Evaluate the message

N = Neutralize the feelings

Look Interested; Get Interested

The best way to look interested when listening to someone is to *get* interested. Networking is about building true relationships. Good questions act as ice-breakers and can effectively make a person feel comfortable.

Get Them Talking About Themselves

At networking events, people tend to cluster around the people they already know. This can be overwhelming when you're new to the event. However, there's often someone else who feels the same way you do. That person, too, is probably staring at his phone or watching and hoping to find someone to talk to.

To be a better listener, you need to get the person talking about himself, listen carefully, and respond appropriately. Listening is not a game, and you should never fake it. You want to avoid those awkward situations.

Approach the lone participant, introduce yourself, and get him talking. Greet him using the name on his badge, if he's wearing one. Ask him what he does and what brought him to the event. Be sure to offer your hand and a firm handshake while saying hello.

Here are some ideas of questions to ask:

- Where are you from?
- What do you do? How long have you been doing it?
- What company/school are you with?
- Have you been to this event before? What do you think of it?
- How did you hear about the event?
- What other events do you attend?

Listen carefully to the answers this person provides. Why did he come to the event? He is probably there to find leads for his business, find potential employers or employees, or simply meet people in his industry.

What follow-up questions can you ask to keep the conversation going? Is there another attendee you should introduce your new contact to? How can you help the two connect? Remember that networking is a two-way street. (Yes, I said it again.)

Use Body Language

When speaking with someone, it helps to give signals that you're listening. Use body language to let that person know that you understand what she's saying and that you're on the same page.

Smiling, nodding, or touching your chin can let someone know you're empathetic. Another technique is to casually mirror the other's movements. If your peer begins to use her hands as she explains details to you, you too can use your hands in a similar pattern combined with an affirming nod.

Be sure to lean in slightly if your peer is sharing personal or important information with you. Your body is a barometer to your listening.

Listen with Your Eyes

Your eyes truly are the windows to your soul. Not only can you detect the emotion the person is speaking with by looking into his eyes, you relay empathy that way. Avoid staring at your colleague's eyes, because doing so can make him feel intimidated or put off. Instead, smile and look at his eyes, and then look down at his hands and return to his eyes to avoid that awkward stare.

Avoid scanning the rest of the room as a person is talking to you. This can be difficult to do if you're the host of a social event; I know this well. But the person talking to you deserves your full attention, so do your best to focus your attention on him.

By using body language and listening with your eyes, you gain someone's confidence that you're listening. By listening attentively, you naturally become interested in what is being said.

Involve Yourself by Responding

You need to remain quiet to allow the other person to relay all the pertinent information to you. Naturally, staying mute the entire time is not ideal. Your colleague will be seeking your approval or some form of feedback as she speaks. Instead of breaking into your own long-winded stories, use verbal signals to let her know you are listening and enjoying your time together. You can do so by saying things like, "Oh yes," "I see," "Interesting," "Go on," and "Please tell me more." Short interjections like these will encourage your peer to continue, which will keep you involved.

When opportunity arises, you should ask follow-up questions to continue engaging her. Some examples follow:

- How did that make you feel?
- What did you do next?
- Why do you think that happened?
- Where were you during this time?
- What would you recommend for next time?
- Do you have an example of this?

You will naturally be involving yourself in the conversation by responding with additional questions. Asking more questions helps to ease the other person by letting her know that you're interested in what she has to say.

Stay on Target

To stay on target, you must not allow yourself to become distracted or bored when someone is speaking to you. As I write this, I picture Doug, the dog in the film *Up*, who is suddenly distracted by a squirrel. Squirrel!

Picture yourself at a networking event. When you ask someone how he is, you expect a brief reply, but that is not always the case. The respondent may reply with a full detailed explanation of how he is, which might take a while.

What do you do?

You asked the question, so you should be prepared to hear the answer. Be polite and listen. If you're standing, avoid crossing your arms. This can make you appear closed and not willing to receive the information. The same can be said for crossing and uncrossing your legs while sitting. Try not to think of your reply before the person has finished speaking, because it can cause your mind to wander. Avoid fidgeting with anything on the table, and resist the temptation to check your phone.

If you find that you're feeling distracted and starting to zone out the respondent, wiggle your toes. It sounds strange, but this works. Wiggling your toes tends to perk you up and make you pay better attention. Once your attention has returned, look into the person's eyes. Remember to listen with your eyes and avoid the squirrels.

> Knock, knock.
>
> Who's there?
>
> Interrupting cow.
>
> Interrupting cow wh...
>
> Moo!!!

My kids still love that joke. (I do too.) Interruptions are serious business, though. You can easily annoy or upset someone speaking to you if you interrupt her. It's easy to lose your patience with someone who gives you every minute detail. But you need to allow the person to speak at her most comfortable pace.

At a networking event recently, I overheard two women speaking. The first woman was telling the other about a new restaurant that had recently opened. The second woman interrupted her to say that she had been there already. The first woman continued explaining what her favorite dish is at the new restaurant, but she was quickly interrupted. The other woman interjected that the dish is fine, but she should really try another, because it is much better. This back and forth went on for several minutes until the first woman walked away looking defeated.

This is not to say that you can't share your stories and opinions too, but you need to learn to listen more than you speak. By continually interrupting the person talking with your own stories or opinions, you end up one-upping them. Imagine the same two women speaking with a small group of people instead. Each time the second lady would interrupt and correct the first, the first would feel more and more embarrassed.

The rule of thumb to stick with is to never interrupt—with the exception of knock-knock jokes, of course.

Test Your Understanding

One company I worked with used to hire expert guest speakers to meet with staff on a range of topics relevant to the business. On one such occasion, a speaker visited who specialized in communication. He raised one point that seemed to resonate with everyone, because we all felt internal communication could use improvement.

He explained that we should aim to listen and repeat direction from our colleagues using phrases like, "So what you're saying...," "I understand; you would like me to...." By repeating instruction, several things occur:

- You test your understanding of the topic matter.
- The person speaking is reassured that you listened and understood the instruction or information.
- You're more likely to be clear on the instruction.
- You'll remember the request by repeating it.

Perhaps your supervisor has pulled you aside to give you important instructions for a task. Instead of simply listening to his directions and returning to your desk, you should repeat the instructions. Here is a little example in homage to the film *Office Space*.

Supervisor: "I need you to remember to file the TPS report by 5:00 p.m. Friday, because Ms. Smith will be returning Monday and will need access to them in order to meet her end-of-day deadline on Tuesday. The TPS report can be found in the shared TPS_X report folder."

Employee: "So what you are saying is the TPS report needs to be filed by 5 p.m. Friday, because Ms. Smith will need them on Monday, and I can find the file in the TPS X drive?"

Supervisor: "That is correct. Thank you."

From my own enhanced listening skills after the presentation, I was amused to notice the phrase "So, what you are saying is..." was iterated hundreds of times over the following weeks by each person in my department. I swear we were the most informed team with the strongest communication skills after we began to use this one simple saying.

Now envision yourself at a networking event meeting a person for the first time. As the person introduces himself to you, it's important to repeat the pertinent information.

You: "It's a pleasure to meet you. Tell me how I can help you."

Attendee: "Well, I'm seeking a job in marketing for a publishing company."

You: "Are you willing to relocate, or would you prefer to find something in the city?"

Attendee: "I just moved my family here, so staying in the city would be ideal."

You: "I understand. I will check around to see if anyone is seeking a marketing person in a publishing company in town. I will follow up with you if I hear of anything."

Attendee: "Perfect! Thank you very much."

Try this the next time you're taking direction from someone or you're being told about some important steps to a task. Testing your understanding also comes in handy in job interviews or sales calls by allowing you an extra moment to be clear on a question before answering it.

Evaluate the Message

At this point in the conversation, you have been actively listening to someone speaking. Perhaps it is your supervisor at your office who has given you instruction for a project, maybe it is a person you just met at a networking event, or it might

be a new contact you're meeting over coffee who may be able to help make some introductions for you.

You need to evaluate the message you've received. This doesn't mean you should stop listening. However, you need to take the information you're given to make a decision to act upon it.

The supervisor has asked you to work this weekend. Evaluate whether you can commit to that. Can you shuffle around your weekend plans to be able to be in the office this Saturday?

The person at the networking event has expressed her difficulty finding job candidates in your city. Evaluate her problem. You know some people who may be perfect candidates; you should offer to introduce them to her.

The coffee date has suggested you contact a small business owner with similar aspirations so you can be properly introduced. Evaluate this suggestion. Yes, you would love to meet other like-minded people.

Don't stop there. You should not only be evaluating *what* is said, but *how* it is said. The body language of the one talking can indicate his feelings behind what he says.

Just as I described that as the listener you need to focus on showing empathy and respect toward the person speaking using your own body language, it's also important to read his body language to determine any underlying messages.

Neutralize the Feelings

Dale Carnegie writes in *How to Win Friends and Influence People*:

> "You can't win an argument. You can't because if you lose it, you lose it; and if you win it, you lose it. Why? Well, suppose you triumph over the other man and shoot his argument full of holes and prove that he is non compos mentis. Then what? You will feel fine. But what about him? You have made him feel inferior. You have hurt his pride. He will resent your triumph."[4]

It will happen—you are going to speak to someone you don't agree with. She may state something that you know is incorrect. The point of the conversation isn't about being right, though; it's about meeting a new contact and hopefully building a relationship. You must neutralize your feelings to be a strong listener.

Remember Names

Have you ever been approached by someone you know but whose name you can't recall? Even worse is when you must introduce two people, but you only remember one of their names. This can be brutally awkward and tremendously embarrassing.

If you have just met, most people will give you a grace period to embarrassingly ask for their name again. Picture the two of us meeting for the first time at a networking event. You introduce yourself to me, and I do my best to remember your name. Here is an example of how the conversation could unfold.

> You: "This is a great event. My name is Greg Wallace."

> Me: "Yes, it's great. It's a pleasure to meet you, Greg. Where are you from?"

Notice that I repeat your name. Then I ask you a question to learn more about you and to attempt to find another way to remember your name.

> You: "I was born in Scotland, but I was raised in the United States."

> Me: "Ah, a distant relative of William Wallace?" said jokingly.

I instantly connect Wallace with William Wallace, the Scottish hero as played by Mel Gibson in the movie *Braveheart*.

> You: "I wish. That would be cool!"

> Me: "What brings you to the event, Greg?"

I repeat your name again, to help it sink into my head.

Meeting someone with a more difficult name can be a great benefit toward helping you recall it. In this case, I would ask you for the spelling of your name and if it has any meaning.

> You: "Hello, it's nice to meet you. My name is Nina Bhatnagar."

> Me: "It's nice to meet you, Nina. How do you spell your surname?"

> You: "B-h-a-t-n-a-g-a-r."

> Me: "It's a beautiful name! Is it Indian?"

> You: "Yes, it is."

> Me: "Nina, does Bhatnagar have any special meaning?"

You can also imagine a silly situation from a person's name. This imaginary scene you dream up can help make the name more memorable.

> You: "Hi there. What a fun networking event!"
>
> Me: "Yes, it is. I'm Dave Delaney. What's your name?"
>
> You: "Abe. Abe Andrews."
>
> Me: "It's nice to meet you, Abe. What do you do for a living?"
>
> You: "I'm a dentist."

I would instantly picture my new friend Abe holding a dental drill, posing in a black-and-white photograph, standing over former president Abraham Lincoln with his mouth wide open.

These are just a few examples of how you can remember a person's name. Repetition and a little creativity can go a long way in helping you achieve this.

A partner in crime can also help you in a bind. A close friend frequents many social events with his wife. Whenever he doesn't remember a person's name, he introduces his wife first, who takes that as a cue to instantly ask for the contact's name. It plays out something like this:

> Husband: "I'm glad to see you again. I would like to introduce you to my wife."
>
> Wife: "Nice to meet you. I'm Debbie. What's your name?"

Remember Faces

The other day I was enjoying a cup of coffee at one of my favorite local cafes. It was a busy day, and the tables, couches, and chairs around me were full. I had my head down staring intently into my computer as I worked. I stopped for a moment, raised my head, and took a sip of my coffee. Just as I did, a woman entered the room and waved enthusiastically to me. For the life of me, I couldn't recall who the waving stranger was, but in an effort not to be rude, I smiled and waved back.

Just as I lowered my hand from my welcoming wave, she approached me. She had a warm smile that was glowing as she got closer to my table. As I made eye contact with her, she walked past me and joined a table of women who had been expecting her. Imagine my embarrassment. I quickly ducked my head back into my computer hoping no one had witnessed the incident.

Has this happened to you, too? I decided to come clean and share my little tale on Facebook. I counted 15 comments from friends who had experienced similar situations. If it has happened to you, know that you are not alone, and at least you were being friendly.

It turned out that this person was a stranger, but sadly I have had panicky moments when someone approached me who looked familiar, but I couldn't remember where I knew him from.

One way to help you remember the faces is to consider your location. If you are in school and see a person you think you know, begin by thinking of the people you know from school. If the person is at an association's networking event, consider whether you know the person from that association or related industry.

Study the faces and physical characteristics of the people you meet. You can often put a name to a face when you practice this while meeting people. For example, Noel may have a large mole on his chin. Mole equals Noel. Rose may have red hair. Red equals Rose. Sometimes it can be more difficult to find a quick connection. Jay may be short, and Jay is a short name. Short equals Jay.

Don't be afraid to ask for a reminder about someone's name. It's far worse to leave the situation without ever knowing the person's name or how you know each other. Sometimes it's best to simply admit defeat and ask the person for a reminder of how you know each other.

Robert H. Nutt shares a fun technique to help train your brain to remember faces in *How to Remember Names and Faces: How to Develop a Good Memory*. He writes:

> *"Go to the movies. It's dark there, and you can forget about yourself thoroughly as you scrutinize the faces on the screen. Analyze the appearances of the actors and actresses, giving particular attention to hair, eyes, ears, noses, mouths. Try to figure out the ages of the different characters; notice their height and their gait. When a close-up flashes on the screen, watch out for wrinkles, moles, and warts. Keep your ears wide open for the quality of the voices..."*[5]

I love this technique because you can do it alone with nobody knowing. You can also do it while riding on a bus, eating in a restaurant, or sitting on a park bench.

To test your proficiency at remembering faces, try the BBC's "Brainsmart" site (www.bbc.co.uk/scotland/brainsmart/games/faces/) and attempt to associate the names with the faces you see. You can begin by memorizing 5 "easy" faces and move on to memorizing 10 and 20 faces. This is a good activity to rehearse before you venture out to a local networking event. Practicing focusing on a person's face and associating it with her name will help you remember the names and faces of the new people that you meet.

Refer to Smart Phones and Social Networks

I have several meetings each week at the cafe I mentioned previously in this chapter, often with people I've never met. As my meeting time arrives and my guest is not present, I begin to wonder if my peer has forgotten the meeting. Then I suddenly realize I don't know what my guest looks like, and my guest doesn't know what I look like.

Blind daters have mastered the art of giving notice to something special to help identify each other, such as wearing a flower in the hair, a bow tie, a top hat, or a monocle. (Hey, that would work, right?) For some reason, business professionals often forget this important step.

Luckily, there are social networks and smart phones you can refer to before the meeting. I often check the LinkedIn or Facebook apps for the profile of the person I'm about to meet to see what he looks like, making it easier to find each other.

As I explained in Chapter 1, "Do Your Homework," by referring to social profiles of the people you're meeting, not only can you find out what they look like, but you can learn more about them so you're fully prepared for the meeting. This knowledge can improve your memory of people by connecting their names with their hobbies or profession.

Gain Trust, Respect, and Knowledge

Stephen R. Covey, author of the classic book *The 7 Habits of Highly Effective People*, famously wrote, "Most people do not listen with the intent to understand; they listen with the intent to reply."[6]

By becoming a better listener, your interactions with people will be more enjoyable and rewarding. You will gain the trust and respect of your peers as they speak with you. Better listening will also leave you more knowledgeable, because you will receive your peer's information and retain it before allowing it to be whisked away through that other ear of yours.

Mastering the art of listening makes you more trustworthy, respected, and smarter, so why wouldn't you seek to improve your listening skills? Nobody is a perfect listener, but it's important to strive to become better. Use the L.I.S.T.E.N. techniques to improve your skills and enrich your relationships.

Endnotes

1. Rankin, Paul T. "The Importance of Listening Ability." *The English Journal*, Vol. 17, No. 8 (Oct. 1928), pp. 623–630. National Council of Teachers of English. www.jstor.org/stable/803100.

2. www.ted.com/talks/julian_treasure_5_ways_to_listen_better.html

3. McKimm, Professor J. *and* Mr. D. Parkin. "Managing the appraisal." *British Journal of Hospital Medicine*, Vol. 70, No. 9. Article 8 (September 2009). http://www.faculty.londondeanery.ac.uk/other-resources.

4. Carnegie, Dale, *How to Win Friends and Influence People* (New York: Simon & Schuster, 2009)

5. Nut, Robert H. *How to Remember Names and Faces: How to Develop a Good Memory* (*Whitefish, Montana*: Kessinger Publishing, LLC., *2005*)

6. Covey, Stephen R. *The 7 Habits of Highly Effective People (New York: Free Press, 2004)*

11

Business Cards That Rock and When to Use Them

With the exception of children, everyone should have a business card, even those between jobs, students, or professionals looking to make a transition. People must promote themselves, not just their businesses. A business card gives a person a quick way to contact you later. It serves as a reminder of who you are, where you met (if the recipient made a note on the card), and why the recipient should follow up later. Your business card can even be a conversation starter, like the classic scene in the frightening film American Psycho.

In the movie, the main character, Patrick Bateman, is sitting around a boardroom table comparing business cards with his colleagues. Bateman is eager to share his new business card. He boasts that its color is bone and the lettering is called Silian Rail. One colleague one-ups him revealing that his card has an eggshell color and uses Romalian type, which impresses the group. Another coworker excites the group with his pale nimbus white

card with raised lettering. Finally, Bateman begins to crack as another workmate has the group in awe with his card. Bateman's inner monologue says, "Look at that subtle off-white coloring. The tasteful thickness of it. Oh my God, it even has a watermark...."[1]

If you have a creative business card, it could very well become the topic of your conversation while you meet people at a networking event, introduce yourself to a new client, or find yourself in a Manhattan skyscraper boardroom among a small group of yuppies, like Patrick Bateman and friends.

Rules of Engagement

Nobody likes the obnoxious guy at the networking event handing out business cards as quickly as a Las Vegas dealer. The whole point to networking is to meet like-minded people who you can help and who may be able to help you one day. Giving and receiving business cards should be something done with consideration, not an invasive act of self-promotion.

Your business card is the perfect way to leave someone with a tangible object to remember you by. Your card will include your contact information so that a person you meet can follow up with you later.

Be tactful and wait for the opportunity to give a person your card when asked for it. If you're enjoying your conversation with this new contact, ask him for his card. He will likely reciprocate and ask for yours in exchange. It's wise to always ask for a card before offering yours.

I was working at a major trade show one year. I entered an exhibitor's booth and began to look around when a slick gentleman approached. Before I could even finish saying hello, he was already trying to sell me on the bells and whistles of his self-proclaimed revolutionary products. He didn't let me get a word in until the end of his bothersome blather, when he asked my name. "Dave," I replied. He then aggressively stuck out his hand to shake mine. When I shook his hand, he slipped me his business card without my expecting it.

As I walked away from his booth feeling violated, I noticed the floor was littered with his business cards. I felt badly for him, especially if he should happen upon the pile of wasted opportunities. I pictured people walking away from his booth whipping his cards away, like David Letterman's classic blue card toss.

When meeting someone new, I always begin by asking questions and being personable. In the book *Career Intelligence*, author Barbara Moses eloquently writes, "Your business card is not an extension of your hand."[2] It's only when the person requests your card that you hand him one. Don't be *that* guy with the cards.

Importance of Knowing Your Audience

An important step in designing a business card (or having one designed) is to know who you will be handing it to. For example, a business card shaped like a ninja star may not win you points at a dental conference, just as your boring white rectangle may be overlooked at a conference on design.

Make your card reflect your personality or your business. If you're an outgoing, extroverted, wild and crazy person, you can probably get away with a louder, more creative card. Figures 11.1 and 11.2 show some creative examples.

Figure 11.1   *Flow Yoga, Vancouver, B.C., Canada.*[3]

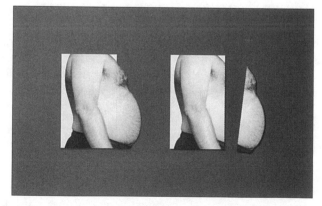

Figure 11.2   *Fitness trainer Zohra Mouhetta: Lose Your Belly by Leo Burnett.*[4]

Who are you? What do you do? What message do you want to relay to the world? Make a card that's appropriate for your industry. Just because you work (or hope

to work) in an industry that's a little on the conservative side, you don't have to create a conservative card. You can still create a business card that reflects your personality, but leave the Bedazzler at home. Take a look at the tasteful card in Figure 11.3 for an example of this. If you work in a creative industry, let your creative side shine by designing a card that your peers will appreciate and remember. (You may still choose to leave the Bedazzler at home.)

Figure 11.3   *Penelope Jones Interior Design.*

Understand that you want the recipient of your card to be impressed with it and at least keep it long enough to reconnect with you by email or LinkedIn later. Naturally, the recipient needs to be impressed with you first.

CREATE A PERSONAL CARD

Remember, as I described in Chapter 3, "Your Home on the Web Needs More Than a Welcome Mat," you may have an occasion to create your own personal card to carry along with your professional card. This is perfect when you connect with someone you have an outside interest with. For example, you may be a musician outside of your daily job and want to connect over your shared interest.

One Card to Rule Them All

I will write more in a moment about having different business cards for various occasions, but before taking the steps to create multiple cards, you must have a single card—a default card you carry at all times. This is the card you will hand

to strangers when the occasion arises. You may use this card at a cocktail party or during a chance encounter, or you may use it for a chance to win burritos for your entire office department. (Admit it; you've done this!)

The card you carry may be your personal card, or it may be a card provided by your employer. The most basic information your card needs is the name of your company or the company you work for (if applicable), your name, job title, email address, phone number, and website address. Your default card may also include your business's logo and your social profile handle for Twitter or LinkedIn if your employer includes it.

Whether it's your personal card or your employer's card, keep in mind that this is your general card, your go-to card. It may also be your only card, and that's fine. Be sure that it is general enough for anyone to receive it and that the contact information is clear and concise.

A Card for the Occasion

You may also choose several different short runs of cards based on special occasions, like industry conferences or trade shows. I've seen cards that include unique mentions of the specific event attended. When you create a card like this, it's wise to also include a unique landing page on your blog or site and have a URL that points there. The page can include a special offer, or the copy can reflect where you met the person, such as at a specific conference. For example, include a message like, "It was great to meet you at XYZ conference. Let's keep in touch." Then add the following fields:

We met at _____

We talked about _____

Follow up _____

Get creative with the fields you choose to include. These act as a fun and useful way for a recipient to remember who you are after the event, plus it encourages them to follow up, because they can actually write a note on the card.

If you're an interior designer, you may want your card to be more stylish and modern for an upcoming design conference. You may have a more masculine appearing card for a conference on home improvements. I hate to sound like I'm generalizing here, but you must be strategic when considering the majority of the people who will receive your card.

Effective Design

I'll be the first to admit it: I'm not a designer. However, I know a good design when I see one, and I know what works well and what doesn't. Your business card should never be too heavy in copy. Instead, the text should be clear and easy to read. Avoid dark font on dark backgrounds and light font on light backgrounds. A creative design should be eye catching and memorable, just like everyone strives to be.

Word of mouth marketer and customer experience designer Saul Colt uses the plain white approach to his business cards, as you see in Figure 11.4. Each of his cards includes just enough information to make you want to learn more. There is only one call to action: a mysterious link.

Figure 11.4   *Saul Colt. www.saul.is/a-good-kisser.*[5]

In plain black typeface, one card reads, "Saul Colt, International Man of Mystery." The card then includes a curious link: www.saul.is/a-man-of-mystery. The link leads you to a page on his site that includes his contact information and a link to a video message. Another of his cards has the same style and reads, "Saul Colt, Good Kisser." It includes the URL www.saul.is/a-good-kisser. Both are fine examples of having some fun with your business cards while understanding who the recipient will be.

Many photographers and other visually creative people use cards from Moo.com, a service that connects with your Flickr, Facebook, Picasa, SmugMug, or Etsy

accounts to pull images from. You choose your favorite photos, and Moo prints each card with a different image of your choosing. Artists and other creative people proudly fan these out like a deck of cards, allowing you to select your favorite image while giving you a quick glimpse of what they're all about.

Personal Photos on Cards

I took an informal poll on Facebook to find out what types of business cards by industry are the worst. The answers included lawyers, private medical professionals, and real estate agents, who won by a landslide.

Why real estate agents? One thing they usually have in common is a photograph, but not necessarily a good one. Are you a real estate agent, lawyer, or private medical professional? Please don't take offense to these results from my unscientific poll. You may actually be inspired, though, to revisit your card and decide to update the photo. However, your photo may be beautiful, and you can disregard this section all together.

I use a photograph on my card, as you will see in Figure 11.5. However, I have the whole photo taking up one side, rather than including it in a small white square. Little white squares are *square*. The photo, taken by Bradley Spitzer, has a dark background, which is perfect for adding my details in a lighter font color over the background. Including a good photo helps the recipient remember who I am.

Figure 11.5   *Photo by Bradley Spitzer.*

In some cases, you shouldn't use a photograph. Larger companies usually don't include photos of the person on the card. Obviously, the company information and contact information are most important. For a company, the logo is likely more imperative than your headshot (to them).

At the end of the day, it's up to you or your employer to decide whether your fetching mug will be affixed to your card. If you decide to include it, I highly recommend using a professional photographer to shoot your headshot and think how the photo can take up the full side of the card, instead of just a little box like so

many others. It doesn't have to be your whole face taking up the card, but it should include you in the photo. For example, my card has a dark background where the photo was taken.

CALL TO ACTION

A *call to action* in marketing means the thing you most want a person to do. Items like a Buy Now button on a website, a Sign Up for Our Email Newsletter message, or a Like Us on Facebook link are all calls to action. What do you hope to achieve with your business card? What's the most important thing you want the recipient to do? Use a call to action to achieve this. Some examples include "Give me a call," "Follow me on Twitter," or "Get a free download."

QR Codes

If you're using your card with a technology, marketing, or advertising crowd, you may decide to use a QR code. A QR code is like a barcode found on just about everything you buy. The QR stands for quick response, because you can scan it using a smart phone. Once scanned, the code can automatically take you to a destination, like your splash page, site, or blog as shown in Figure 11.6. You can also configure it to automatically add your personal information from your card to the recipient's contact list on her phone.

Figure 11.6 *Stephanie Obodda.*

The verdict is undecided at this time about QR codes. These codes are continuously being tested by marketing departments on signage, product packaging, and more. If you haven't noticed them before reading this, you'll likely see them frequently now. There are some downsides to QR codes, which can result in the codes not being scanned. The downsides follow:

- People don't know what they are.
- Some smart phones don't come equipped to read them. You need to install an app to achieve this.
- Poorly designed or displayed codes don't scan properly, resulting in user frustration.

There are plenty of free sites to create a quick QR code: qrcode.kaywa.com and qrstuff.com. If you decide to use a QR code, here are a few tips:

- Make the QR code as large as possible without interfering with the rest of the content on the card.
- Print a draft of the card and test it with multiple QR code scanning apps. Search for QR Code in your app store.
- Never depend on the QR code to be the single call to action. Not everybody will scan it. Provide another call to action in addition to the QR code.
- Use Google's URL Builder to track the success of the code. Learn more at http://bit.ly/GoogleURLBuilder2.
- Use Bit.ly to shorten the tracking code generated from Google's URL Builder. You can add a plus sign (+) to the end of the Bit.ly link later to review additional analytics like clicks and geographical information.
- Make the QR code link to something unique and original. Create a special video and link to it from the code. Be sure the content that you direct people to is optimized to be read on a mobile device. You can test how your landing page appears using www.mobilephoneemulator.com or any other mobile emulator.

NFC Chips

Near-field communication (NFC) chips are beginning to be used in business cards to create a truly interactive experience. NFC chips will make your business card work similarly to a security pass card or credit card. A user simply taps your card to his device, and your contact information is automatically transferred. You keep your card, and the recipient gets your information.

Imagine yourself at a networking event. You meet someone for the first time, and she asks for your card. You ask her to take out her smart phone and automatically send her your contact information by tapping your card against her phone. You can also have the card launch a video or site on her phone if you prefer. Pretty cool, right?

NFC cards can also be reprogrammed, so you can configure them to do different things. For example, you may want to send your contact information with a note about which conference you met at to help the recipient remember. Moo.com has a good demo on its site at http://us.moo.com/nfc/.

Some smart phones are already set up to receive information from NFC chips, but not all manufacturers have decided to adopt the technology. The cost for NFC cards right now is quite high. NFC is certainly something to watch for in the future.

Apps to the Rescue

Remember the days when you had to use a manual hand-held business card scanner to scan the information from each of the cards you received after an event? You would cross your fingers and hope that the software would be able to render the text from the cards. This was a major pain, as was trying to scan cards with crossed fingers!

I know I already used Apple's popular catch phrase, "There's an app for that," in this book, but it's so good I have to use it again. The following are applications I recommend that you download and use to record the information from the pile of business cards you collect during your networking efforts.

CardMunch by LinkedIn

CardMunch is a business card scanning application. It's by far the best one I've used, because actual humans on the other end transcribe the information. Once the card has been scanned, the information can be forwarded and saved to your phone. You can also press the Connect button to instantly send a LinkedIn connection request. However, I prefer using the envelope icon to automatically compose an email invitation to connect on LinkedIn. Remember my advice from Chapter 4, "Grow Your Network Before You Need It: LinkedIn." Always edit the email to make it more personal.

CardMunch boasts 100% accuracy for business cards you scan. If you long for the old days of a Roledex on your desk, you can turn the phone landscape and manually flip through the cards you have scanned, all without the paper cuts.

Hello by Evernote

Evernote is the popular app known as "the tool to help you remember everything." The company launched a new app called Hello, which provides a perfect way to scan business cards and write notes about the people you meet.

A quick scan of a business card, and Hello will import the details from Facebook and LinkedIn, making connecting online after meeting offline a breeze. I recommend using Hello after a meeting or interview, so you can record your notes about the people you met and the details from the meeting.

Hello syncs the information automatically with your Evernote account. A basic account is free. There is a paid version for additional storage and options.

Bump

The innovative, free Bump application is one I've used for a few years now. It's especially handy when networking with a technology-savvy group who likely use the app, too. You bump your phone against another's, and your virtual business cards are magically transferred to each other's phones. Even more impressive is that you can transfer information from iPhone to Android and vice versa.

Configure your Bump card with all your pertinent information like a headshot, phone numbers, email, URL, and address, plus social networks like Twitter, LinkedIn, Facebook, and Google+.

Bump's most recent update has added the capability of transferring photos and files by simply bumping your phone against your computer. Consider doing this after an event where you have snapped many photos and want to back them up quickly.

I recommend reviewing the people you met using Bump from time to time, especially after a large event. You can press the speech bubble icon to see your activity of who you bumped and when and where it occurred. From this screen, you can send a chat message or look at their profile to find other ways to follow up.

Voice Recorder

There are plenty of voice recording apps on the market. Most smart phones come with a default one included, but you can find ones that are tailored to your needs by searching your favorite app store.

As an iPhone user, I use the regular Evernote app or iTalk Recorder. Both apps are perfect for recording voice memos to yourself. Each time I meet someone new, I add their business card information to my contact list and try to record some

audio to remember details about how we met and what we talked about. One question I ask myself is, "How I can help this person?"

Alternatives if You Don't Use a Smart Phone

Smart phone adoption continues to rise in the United States and around the world. However, it's fair to say that not everyone has one yet. An alternative to the business card scanning apps I've mentioned is either manually entering the information into a spreadsheet or using a paid service like Shoeboxed.com. You send the company your business cards, and the company scans them and enters them into a spreadsheet, which you then import into your address book later.

Follow-Up

What good is exchanging contact information if you don't take the next step and contact the person? Following up is just as important as having a great business card. When you return to your office or home after an interview, networking event, or conference, be sure to review the business cards you received and the notes you recorded.

What are the next steps? How can you help each person? Even if you don't have a need to reach out directly to the person, you should send him a request to connect on LinkedIn, with a brief personalized note reminding him how you met and what you talked about.

In Chapter 12, "We Live and Die by Our Database," I write more about databases. They serve as a vital part of organizing and keeping track of your new network contacts.

Personal Style

Business cards should reflect who you are and what you do for a living. Consider making an additional "personal" card and use it when an opportunity arises. Create cards that complement your style and that remind people who you are. Be sure to include a call to action on your card, so the recipient knows what to do with it.

Stay organized by scanning or manually entering the card information from the people you meet. Make notes about how you met, and set reminders of when you should follow up.

You can create a wild and crazy card, but be sure you are using it among wild and crazy people. A card made of cement may go over well at a construction or

architecture conference, as would a card made of meat be an instant favorite at a restaurant tradeshow. However, those two types of cards would probably be less successful with different crowds.

And yes, you can get a card made from concrete or meat! Google it, and you'll see I'm not making this stuff up!

Endnotes

1. *American Psycho*. Dir. Mary Harron. Perfs. Christian Bale. 2000. DVD. Lions Gate Films. 2000.

2. Moses, Barbara. *Career Intelligence* (San Francisco: Berrett-Koehler Publishers, 1998)

3. www.boredpanda.com/creative-business-cards-part3/

4. www.ibelieveinadv.com/2009/04/zohra-mouhetta-lose-your-belly/

5. www.saul.is/a-good-kisser

12

We Live and Die by Our Database

We're deeply connected people. Thanks to social networking sites, we're more connected today than we've ever been before. British anthropologist and evolutionary psychologist Robin Dunbar famously determined that people can only manage up to 150 relationships, otherwise known as Dunbar's Number. So how is it possible to juggle thousands of relationships?

Dunbar writes in his book, How Many Friends Does One Person Need?, "Just as a computer's ability to handle complex tasks is limited by the size of its memory and processor, so the brain's ability to manipulate information about the constantly changing social domain may be limited by the size of its neocortex."[1] When you get right down to it, your brain cannot handle balancing more than 150 connections.

Just because you max out at 150 relationships doesn't mean you can't be connected to more people, though.

What it does mean is that you must be more diligent with how you manage these relationships, so your attention is directed to the right people at the right time. Juggling so many relationships can often feel as stressful as a juggler tossing flaming torches into the air, hoping not to miss. You, too, hope not to miss dates and important life events of the people in your network.

You're probably guilty of having connections to people on social networks who you hardly ever (perhaps never) interact with. Everyone is. Not everyone wants to reconnect with childhood friends or people they dated in high school and college. You accepted your boss's friend request on Facebook, but you may not want to interact with her outside the office.

Today, your career not only depends on who you're connected with, but how you manage those relationships. What good is having a massive contact list if you never use it to connect with anyone? Reach out to your contacts!

In Chapter 1, "Do Your Homework," I wrote about a free spreadsheet (bit.ly/NBNsimpledb) you can download from new-networking.com. The spreadsheet is a simple document for you to insert the contacts you meet, their contact information, and notes about how you should follow up and what the outcome was from following up. This is a good way to get started for free. There are also free and paid solutions to help you organize your contacts, which I will write more about later in this chapter.

Size Doesn't Matter

I would rather have a network of 50 knowledgeable and reliable contacts than 1,000 who have forgotten I exist. Quality over quantity is important to remember as you read this book and consider your networking efforts. As you build a solid database, be sure to refer to this idea frequently to remember who you should be reconnecting with and who you can introduce to one another. If you can't find opportunities to help a person in your database now, you may be able to later.

Being connected to many people can be helpful through your career, but having true relationships with a smaller number will be more rewarding. Don't be like that Las Vegas dealer chucking cards to everyone you see. Be strategic in who you connect with, and always determine how you can help them first. If you don't know at first, ask them. Everybody appreciates it when you extend a helping hand. What goes around comes around in networking—always.

Caring For and Nurturing Your Database

In the book, *Trust Agents*, by Julien Smith and Chris Brogan, they write about the lesson Chris learned from Vonage cofounder and 140 Characters Conference

founder Jeff Pulver. Jeff told Chris, "One's personal database is an asset as valuable as gold, if nurtured and maintained." Jeff also coined the phrase, "You live or die by your database."[2]

Do your best to build your list in one place. I realize you will have different connections with different people on different social networks, but it's important to try to bring them all together if possible. By having all your contacts in one place, like the spreadsheet I provide or a more extensive database software, you can easily refer to it for quick review or a deeper search.

By reviewing your database periodically, you can find people in your network to reconnect with. Do this by sharing an interesting article that you think they will enjoy, or offer to introduce them to another contact you think may result in a beneficial relationship. Wish them a happy birthday should their birthday be approaching. If you both belong to the same group on LinkedIn, Facebook, or Community on Google Plus, you may want to reach out to discuss an interesting topic. The same applies to whether you follow them on Twitter. A quick mention is a nice way to publicly say hello, or consider sending them a direct message if they are following you back.

Software Suggestions

CRM is a popular acronym that describes software to help manage your relationships. *CRM* stands for Customer Relationship Management, or in the case of networking, it stands for Contact Relationship Management. When it comes to software to manage your database, there are many different options on the market. Some are expensive and built for teams, whereas others are free or inexpensive and made for individuals. Ideally, the software will help you keep your contact information up to date, easily searchable, and backed up. You will want to use it to add notes about the most recent encounters, ways you can help someone, or ways they can help you. The following are some free or inexpensive services to help keep you and your database in good shape.

Nimble

Nimble.com is a well-liked social CRM service. You can use it by connecting your email accounts and social networks. Each day you get an email that shows updates for your connections, such as birthdays (info from Facebook) and new job positions (info from LinkedIn). It includes a section called "Engagement Opportunities" that ties in recent social opportunities for you to reach out and say hello, like new Twitter followers, mentions, and retweets.

I love Nimble because it provides a strong contact management system, plus it ties in each social channel. The daily updates that I mentioned also provide a good

reason for you to reach out to members of your network. Nimble is a good choice if you're looking for a good all-in-one CRM.

WriteThat.Name

One of the biggest challenges of keeping your contact list organized is updating your network's personal information when people change companies, job titles, or other contact information. I've found WriteThat.Name an impressive solution to this challenge.

If you use Gmail, GoogleApps, Outlook, or Lotus Notes, or if your company uses SalesForce or Highrise, you're in luck. WriteThat.Name scans your incoming emails and records the information in each person's email signature. It then automatically updates each contact's information as it detects changes. If you choose, it can also alert you to each change and you can manually accept the update. The emails help keep track of each member of your network's changes, giving you a reason to reach out with an email to check in to see how a member is enjoying her new job, for example.

Gmail and Outlook

I realize that not everyone uses Gmail or Outlook for email. However, I've found that many people who do depend on them to keep their contacts organized. Gmail has a powerful search built in to its email service. (I would expect nothing less; it's by Google, after all.) Outlook also comes equipped with a good search tool. You can create specific folders to archive messages based on who the email is sent from or the contents within like keywords and terms. By creating Gmail filters or Outlook rules, you can easily automate the process of organizing your mail to then search easily later. By doing so, you can quickly refer back to the recent (or archived) conversations you had with your contacts. Keeping your contacts information up to date and the conversations archived helps you to be organized.

Boomerang

One of my favorite add-ons for Gmail or Outlook is called Boomerang (www.baydin.com). Once installed, Boomerang allows you to schedule your replies, which can be handy if you don't want to send a reply right away. The best feature, though, is the ability to push a message back to the top of your inbox to remind you to follow up. Although Boomerang doesn't make changes to your database per se, it does help to manage your relationships by reminding you to follow up. For example, if you introduced two contacts to one another, why not remind yourself to follow up in a few weeks?

LinkedIn

LinkedIn is another obvious option to refer to regularly and keep your database fresh. You should consider tagging your connections with common words to help you keep track of their profession. For example, I may tag George Brown as a "developer." Then when I have contacts asking if I know a good developer, I can quickly search by using the tag to find all developers in my network.

Go to your Connections section on LinkedIn and choose any connection. Under their information, you will see Tags. Choose Edit Tags and select a tag from the drop-down menu or add your own by clicking the + symbol.

I recommend using the LinkedIn app once a day to briefly look through your connection's updates and news. If you opt in for the email updates from LinkedIn, you are also alerted when a connection has left a company or changed a role within a company. This may be the perfect opportunity for you to reach out and offer congratulations on the promotion.

Choose What Works for You

There are many different CRM solutions on the market to help you keep your network contacts organized. If you have a budget and want to take your database management to the next level, I recommend looking at one of the following:

- **Infusionsoft**—Infusionsoft.com
- **Contactually**—Contactually.com
- **BatchBook**—BatchBook.com
- **FullContact**—FullContact.com
- **Plaxo**—Plaxo.com
- **HighRise**—HighRisehq.com

Choose the service that works best for you to manage. Reach out to say hello to your contacts, share an article, or make an introduction from time to time. Be sure to record these encounters, so you keep track of the last time you connected. Note what the outcome was, whether they wrote back to say thank you, and whether you heard back at all. Keeping relationships alive is just as important as having them in the first place.

Protecting Your Database

I was an early user of Twitter. I began using the service in February 2007. Back then, *social media marketing* was not yet a term, and few jobs specialized in it. As an early adopter of Twitter, I was a huge fan. I loved the simple interface and the

brevity of the messages. The speed of interacting and finding people to interact with was second to none. Microblogging was becoming more popular than blogging for many users. I even wondered if microblogging would be the death of the personal blog. (It wasn't.)

By August 2008, I had accumulated thousands of followers. I reciprocated by following most of them back, too. The daily interactions were something I looked forward to. I was using Twitter far more frequently than Facebook, LinkedIn, MySpace (popular back then), or even email. I was making real friends on Twitter, many I am still in touch with today. Then the unthinkable happened: My account was suspended.

Naturally, I freaked out. I was not breaking any rules, and I wasn't using Twitter in any suspicious way. As it turned out, several other friends had their accounts wrongly suspended. It took a couple of days to sort out the mess and get our accounts active again. I never did learn why it happened in the first place, but it served as a major wake-up call. **You don't own your contact list when you use a free social networking service.**

Backing Up

My experience of getting locked out of my Twitter account reminded me that I needed to be vigilant about finding ways to back up my social networks. Unfortunately, this isn't always an easy or even successful task, because social networks don't provide alternative ways to contact people such as email address or phone numbers. Obviously, this makes sense in an effort to protect your information. Still, it's troubling when you find yourself suddenly cut off from the network you invested so much time and effort into building.

The following are the steps you should take to back up the information available from each of the most popular social networks. I will also write more about the importance of email newsletters and why you should invest in a service like Emma, MailChimp, or ExactTarget to start building your list sooner than later.

Backing Up Facebook

Did you know you can export your photos, videos, and updates from your wall, notes, events, friends' names, and private messages from Facebook? You can. Many of your important photos and videos may only live on Facebook. Perhaps crucial planning discussions took place through direct Facebook messages. It's important to have a copy of these separate from the social networking site. This backup file includes your friends' names with their email addresses if they make them accessible. Even if only a few do, it's important to back up all your Facebook archive.

To download an archive of your Facebook profile, log in, click the gear icon in the top-right corner of the page, and choose Account Settings. You see an option to download a copy of your Facebook data at the bottom of the page.

Once downloaded, the file includes all your Facebook profile content. When you open the downloaded files, you find one called index.html. Run this, and you see a basic page of your Facebook information with your name and profile picture. You can choose Friends and see a long list of all of your friends alphabetically; note that only some have an email address included.

The easiest way to quickly and simply back up your Facebook friends (the ones with their email addresses) is to use a free YahooMail account. Once logged in, choose Contacts and Import Contacts. Click the Facebook icon. You may need to log into Facebook. Once you have imported your friends' email addresses and names from Facebook, you can download them as a CSV file from your Yahoo contacts and import them to your database.

Backing Up Twitter Tweets

Not everyone realizes that Twitter provides you with the option to archive your tweets. This is wise to do from time to time for archival purposes. You never know when you might want to revisit a conversation or link you shared with your followers.

Log in to Twitter and choose Account, and then scroll to the bottom of the page. There you should find a button to request your archive. Upon completion, you will receive an email with a file. Once you open it and run the index.html file, you can see all your tweets in chronological order.

Downloading this doesn't give you each follower's contact information. However, this will be good to refer back to so you can track your communication history with your followers. Not to mention, it serves as a wonderful nostalgic look back at your own history on Twitter. I bet you'll find people there you haven't heard from in some time. My archive went back to February 2007. It was fun to look back and see who I spoke with most often then. Reflecting on my earliest contacts on Twitter inspired me to reach out to rekindle some of those relationships.

Backing Up LinkedIn

As I mentioned in Chapter 4, "Grow Your Network Before You Need It: LinkedIn," one thing I love about LinkedIn is the easy ability to export contacts. Consider your LinkedIn backup to be your most important one, because it contains the contact information of much of your network. From the Connections tab, scroll to the bottom and choose Export Contacts. Download the spreadsheet and

keep it in a safe place. The most important aspect of LinkedIn's export is that it includes all your contact's information: name, company, title, URL, address, email, and phone number. That's important, because this is your professional network, and these are your future employers, customers, clients, investors, and industry peers. Go download your connections now. I'll be here when you return.

Creating Email Newsletters

I don't expect that every person reading this book will create a personal email newsletter. However, email is the best way to secure your network's contact information. As I've explained, you can't download your Twitter follower's contact information, and your Facebook friend's information can be limited depending on his privacy settings. It's also difficult or impossible to download and back up the email addresses of your Pinterest, Instagram, or Flickr friends. You can download your LinkedIn connections' contact information, but what if this changes in the future? Remember, you don't own your contact list when you use a free social networking site.

By creating an email newsletter, you strive to build a list from members of all of your social networks and professional contacts combined. By doing this, you manage the list—specifically the names and email addresses of your contacts. This means you always have access to this information and are not dependent on a social network.

Three popular email marketing companies are Emma (MyEmma.com), ExactTarget (ExactTarget.com), and MailChimp (MailChimp.com). Take some time to consider whether you want to create an email newsletter that provides benefits to your friends, fans, and followers. Think of several reasons to encourage your network to sign up for your newsletter. Perhaps you want to share your content that you're creating (see Chapter 8, "Content Is the Glue That Binds Us Together") or promote an upcoming event you're organizing (see Chapter 9, "If You Build It, They Will Come: Organizing Events"). Use your email newsletter to keep your network informed. Every month you should export your newsletter recipient list and back it up. Email addresses are sacred, so be sure to keep your backup in a safe place.

Checking Back, Checking In

From time to time, review your database and the people in it. This process is a good way to reflect upon who you know and who you need to check back or check in with.

Open your spreadsheet of contacts and trim some of the unneeded columns such as job title and addresses, so it is easily printable. Make sure the borders are showing, so your eyeballs don't pop out of your head trying to read the content on the paper. Make it alphabetical by last name and print it. (Sorry, trees.)

Grab a highlighter, a pen, and a cup of coffee or tea. Is it a nice day outside? Take a seat under the sun and begin reviewing your printout. Highlight the names of the people you enjoy the most and who you have not heard from in a while. It's time to reconnect, revive a conversation, or simply check in to see how someone is doing. Rekindle stagnant relationships by reaching out. Let people know what you're up to in your career, but be sure to ask them the same. Start the dialogue and see where it goes.

Use your spreadsheet to take notes about when you followed up and what the outcome was. When should you follow up again? One month? Six months? At the end of the year? Set a follow-up reminder in your calendar, so you don't miss it. This may seem overwhelming, but it's a good place to start. Keep your database up to date. Refer to it frequently, and find a reason to reconnect or to follow up.

I sent a custom message to many of my contacts at the beginning of the year. I wanted to write to check in, give them a brief professional update, and find out how I may be able to help them. By doing so, I received three new clients in January alone. In addition, I scheduled many coffee chats, telephone calls, and Google Hangouts. It was good to get reacquainted with people I hadn't heard from in some time. Consider doing the same and check back in with your network.

Change Is Guaranteed

It's impossible for you to predict your career path. When I reflect upon the different jobs and employers I've had over the years, I'm flabbergasted with the change. Some change makes sense when you look back, while other changes are unexpected. Any way you cut it, change is guaranteed.

It's crucial that you cultivate your relationships today. Think beyond the here and now when growing your network; think long term. Your professor today may become your employer or customer later. Your coworker may become your cofounder. Your top client where you work may end up recruiting you to her company. Just because someone can't help you today doesn't mean that person will always be unable to help you. Keep your database up to date and organized.

Tending to your network is paramount. Check back in with your connections and offer to help them when possible. Look for opportunities to reach out and offer a helping hand, endorse or write recommendations on LinkedIn, send an email to say hello, or pick up the phone. Record your interactions in your database, and make notes of how you helped or how they may help you.

Avoid being overwhelmed with the tools you choose to keep your network database intact. Go as basic as you need (my downloadable spreadsheet: http://bit.ly/NBNsimpledb) or as advanced as you choose. The important thing is that you have a database to refer to and you update it frequently. You live or die by your database.

Endnotes

1. Dunbar, Robin. *How Many Friends Does One Person Need? Dunbar's Number and Other Evolutionary Quirks.* Cambridge: Harvard University Press (2010).

2. Brogan, Chris, and Julien Smith. *Trust Agents*, pp. 170. Hoboken: Wiley and Sons (2010).

13

Strong Relationships Lead to Success

The act of business networking is crucial to a long and fruitful career. Not only can connecting with new people broaden your professional network, it can (and usually does) result in new friendships.

It's up to you to take the steps to meet new people. Use social networks to meet people and get better acquainted with the ones you already know. Go offline and attend or organize events. By meeting new people, you enrich your life, enhance your career, and ultimately grow your network.

In 1943, psychologist Abraham Maslow famously released a study titled "A Theory of Human Motivation."[1] His study concludes that humans shift across five steps that define needs they seek to become "self-actualized" people. The steps are commonly illustrated using a pyramid shape, as you see in Figure 13.1.

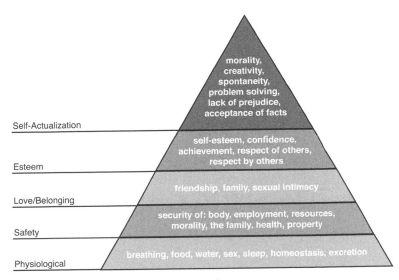

Figure 13.1 *Maslow's Hierarchy of Needs.[2]*

As you see in the diagram, the first step (at the bottom) encompasses physiological needs like air, food, water, and sex. The next tier up involves safety with items like security of body, finances, and family. The final three tiers are directly connected to the act of networking. In fact, if a new job or client is a result of networking, you may also achieve the level of safety as a result.

Maslow's third level is Love/Belonging. While networking may not result in love necessarily (although it could), it certainly will gain you new friendships over time. I've made new friends from organizing networking events like Nashcocktail and Geek Breakfast. I've also made new friends from attending other networking events. To achieve Maslow's third level of needs, you need to get out of your house or office and meet new people. Refer to Chapter 1, "Do Your Homework," to find events and get out there.

The fourth level of Maslow's Hierarchy of Needs includes self-esteem, confidence, and respect of and by others. By reviewing who is attending and perhaps connecting with them online before an event, you ease the nervousness you may feel about attending. By using the skills I shared with you in Chapter 10, "Listen Better. Remember More," you become a better listener, which can help you develop your confidence as you approach new people and start conversations. Your confidence is also enhanced by the trust and respect you receive from the people you meet using your improved listening skills. Even if you are an introvert, you still need to network to improve your career.

The final stage of Maslow's Hierarchy of Needs is Self-Actualization. This step includes morality, creativity, spontaneity, and an acceptance of facts. In other words, you become one with yourself and accept yourself for who you are. Here is a brief personal story related to this.

During one of my networking events, a friend pulled me aside and said that I had missed my calling. Puzzled, I asked him what he meant by this statement. He went on to explain that it was clear to him how I became energized when networking, and he noticed how I loved to be a connector who brings people together. I've written this book for you to learn from the lessons I've absorbed over the years because of my passion for networking. It was this conversation—during a networking event—that made me realize I must continue exploring this topic. I need to share what I learn along the way, while bringing people together as I have over the years. I experienced a degree of self-actualization as Maslow defined it.

Self-actualization for you will probably be different. It could be a massive shift in your career, which may come from spending time meeting people via social networks or in-person events. You may hand a person your personal business card sharing your interest in music. This could result in your forming a band with the person you meet, causing your career to take a complete turn in a different direction.

Much of Maslow's Hierarchy of Needs can be accomplished by dedicating time to networking online and offline. Just as Figure 13.1 indicates, each step can lead closer to self-actualization. Each step aside from the physiological needs can be met in part by meeting new people and growing relationships. Use networking as a way to meet Maslow's steps and to get yourself closer to a state of self-actualization.

Meeting in Real Life

While you use online tools to connect more today than ever before, you still need to unplug and connect in person with those online friends. The tools and techniques you use to meet new people online will inevitably change as social networks mature and new services and tools emerge, but the essence of how you connect shall remain the same when doing so in person.

Can you think of someone you met online and what it felt like when you met in person for the first time? Aside from dating, I bet the moment was joyous. The feeling is often exciting and happy. Once you exchange those high-fives, handshakes, or hugs, your relationships changes. It grows. This is what in real life (IRL) is all about.

One of my favorite memories of meeting online friends in real life was in Kingston, Ontario, in the summer of 2006. The first PAB (Podcasters Across Borders) conference was taking place. My wife and I had been podcasting for a year at this point, but this was the first time we would meet many of our listeners and fellow podcasters. It was an absolutely wonderful time putting people to the voices of the many podcasts I listened to. Close friendships were made that weekend as online friends connected in person, which resulted in even stronger, longer-lasting relationships.

Today it is easier than ever to create your own groups dedicated to a topic of interest. By using online tools like Facebook groups, Google+ communities, or LinkedIn groups, you can gather like-minded people together in one place online to discuss and share thoughts on matters you relate to. As the group matures, I recommend you take your group to the next level by meeting offline IRL if possible.

When you organize the meet-up (or conference in the case of PAB), you become the connector. You're the person providing true value to your attendees and sponsors (when applicable). Bob Goyetche, Mark Blevis, Cathy Bobkowicz, and Andrea Ross did this by giving podcasters a place to congregate, share ideas, and learn from one another at PAB. I will be eternally grateful for their hard work and dedication to PAB. Follow your passions and consider creating an original event or conference. Even a small meet-up is worthwhile if you're bringing people together and acting as a connector.

I can speak firsthand of the warm feeling I experience when I see people meeting for the first time or old friends and colleagues reconnecting at my monthly networking events. If you choose to start your own event, I would love to hear about it. Be sure to visit new-networking.com and share your event and the story behind it with the group.

They Will Use the Web to Learn About You

The future is online. For most, the present is, too. This is why I stressed in Chapter 3, "Your Home on the Web Needs More Than a Welcome Mat," that you must stake your ground on the Web. Buy your personal URL and point it to a splash page like About.me or Flavors.me. You may also consider newer services like Populr.me, which provides you with a static landing page you can personalize. Better yet, create your space using a blog and share your insights and knowledge with your visitors. When you meet someone at an event and strike up a good conversation, you can bet that person will go online to learn more about you and to get better connected by sending you a friend request or by following you. Never forget that employers, recruiters, and anyone seeking more information about you will also pay you a visit online first.

Remember that the content you create online should be optimized for search engines. Always write for humans first and robots second. You do need to consider the bots though, because they will be scanning your content for keywords and terms, which will improve your results in search engines and resume scanning software. SEO will remain an important topic in the future, as will your social connections and peer recommendations. This is why I urge you to make LinkedIn endorsements and write recommendations for the people you've worked or studied with.

Recruiters commonly research candidates by searching their social network profiles. I believe they will be more suspicious of a person who has no digital footprint than someone who has an abundance of content online, even if that content includes embarrassing photos from college. Remember, it's better not to have those embarrassing photos online in the first place. Still, I believe recruiters will think it odd to search a candidate and find nothing online. Use the ideas I've provided you throughout this book to establish yourself online with great content. You don't have to spend hours a day on social networks, but you should have a presence so visitors can learn more about you and say hello.

Update your business card or personal business card with your URL and make it reflect who you are and what you do. Always carry a few cards with you when you are out, because you never know who you may meet. And, of course, carry plenty of cards when you plan to attend an event or conference. It's better to have too many cards than too few.

When you plan to attend an event, you should do your homework first, like I have written in Chapter 1. Do a little research to see who will be attending and connect with them before the event, or make a note to try to seek them out during the event. By using your Facebook or Twitter account to log in to event planning services like Meetup, Eventbrite, and Plancast, you will be able to see who among your network will be attending. You may also choose to visit your friends' profiles to see what other events they plan to attend in the near future. By reviewing the events your network members will be attending, you may find other events to go to. Why not reach out to your contacts directly and ask them for more details about the event? This works both ways—other attendees will take a look at your profile to learn more about you, too. Be ready for people to find you online and ensure that they like what they see.

Networking for Introverts

I know not everyone is keen to meet strangers in person or online. It can be an especially daunting experience at a crowded event where you know no one. I mentioned connecting your social networks with event planning sites, because you can see who among your friends may be attending an event you want to try. Moral support is always appreciated.

Still, being an introvert can be tough. I know this from the conversations I've had with friends who experience this. The high-fives, hugs, and handshakes can be just enough to make an introvert turn and bolt from an event. You're not alone in this feeling.

In Chapter 10, I mentioned that even if you feel alone at a networking event, you're not. The truth, though, is that humans seek one another. Even self-proclaimed

loners want company. You are reading this book and have come this far because you realize the importance of connecting with new people and growing your network of like-minded individuals.

The next time you plan to attend a networking event and you feel apprehensive, consider these tips to help ease you into the moment:

- Check to see who you know that is attending the event before you go. Review Chapter 1 for some tips.

- Ask the host for an introduction to someone in your area of expertise or interest.

- Approach a small group of people speaking, make eye contact, and smile. Chime in, but don't interrupt. Take the first step by introducing yourself.

- Find a single person and approach her. Use my tips in Chapter 10 to strike up a conversation.

- Start a conversation with a sponsor or official member of the group's organization. This person will be happy to tell you more and learn more about you.

- Prepare yourself with your personal pitch and some questions before you attend the event. A short script can help you ease into a conversation.

- Decide when to call it a night. It's perfectly fine to leave an event early. Be proud of yourself for mustering up the courage to attend in the first place. If you only stay for 30 minutes and speak to one person at your first networking event, try to stay longer the next time and speak with two people. Small steps are better than no steps at all.

Rekindling Conversations

Not everything fits into your database. You couldn't possibly log every Twitter direct message or Facebook chat. Not only would this be a laborious undertaking, but it would be extremely time consuming. The more places you carry conversations, the easier it is to accidentally forget to reply or miss an opportunity to follow up. It's a good habit to check your private messages from time to time to see if you need to follow up and rekindle your relationships.

In Twitter, take a look at direct messages (DMs). These are the people you have had private interactions with and are likely among your closest contacts. Scroll through your DMs and review recent conversations. Do the same using Facebook messages. Take it a step further and review your text messages on your phone. Go back as far as you can and look at the conversations you've had. Do you have

opportunities to reach back out or to follow up? Perhaps you can share an article of interest or offer to make an introduction to one of your LinkedIn contacts. The answer probably lies within the messages.

What You Should Do Now

This book should not end when you reach the last word. It should just begin as you take my guidance and put it into action. Sharing your stories with other readers by joining The New Business Networking group at www.new-networking.com will encourage them to do this, too. Networking is about finding like-minded people and connecting. Why not use this book as a reason to connect in the first place?

By meeting new people, you enrich your life, enhance your career, and ultimately grow your network. Review your network from time to time and find ways to offer to help members. Networking is a two-way street. There, I said it again. :)

Endnotes

1. http://psychclassics.yorku.ca/Maslow/motivation.htm

2. http://en.wikipedia.org/wiki/Maslow's_hierarchy_of_needs

Index

Que®
Biz-Tech Series

Straightforward Strategies and Tactics for Business Today

The **Que Biz-Tech series** is designed for the legions of executives and marketers out there trying to come to grips with emerging technologies that can make or break their business. These books help the reader know what's important, what isn't, and provide deep inside know-how for entering the brave new world of business technology, covering topics such as mobile marketing, microblogging, and iPhone and iPad app marketing.

- Straightforward strategies and tactics for companies who are either using or will be using a new technology/product or way of thinking/ doing business

- Written by well-known industry experts in their respective fields— and designed to be an open platform for the author to teach a topic in the way he or she believes the audience will learn best

- Covers new technologies that companies must embrace to remain competitive in the marketplace and shows them how to maximize those technologies for profit

- Written with the marketing and business user in mind—these books meld solid technical know-how with corporate-savvy advice for improving the bottom line

 Visit **quepublishing.com/biztech** to learn more about the **Que Biz-Tech series**

FREE
Online Edition

Safari
Books Online

Your purchase of **New Business Networking** includes access to a free online edition for 45 days through the **Safari Books Online** subscription service. Nearly every Que book is available online through **Safari Books Online**, along with thousands of books and videos from publishers such as Addison-Wesley Professional, Cisco Press, Exam Cram, IBM Press, O'Reilly Media, Prentice Hall, Sams, and VMware Press

Safari Books Online is a digital library providing searchable, on-demand access to thousands of technology, digital media, and professional development books and videos from leading publishers. With one monthly or yearly subscription price, you get unlimited access to learning tools and information on topics including mobile app and software development, tips and tricks on using your favorite gadgets, networking, project management, graphic design, and much more.

Activate your FREE Online Edition at
informit.com/safarifree

STEP 1:   Enter the coupon code: YBAAYYG.

STEP 2:   New Safari users, complete the brief registration form.
            Safari subscribers, just log in.

If you have difficulty registering on Safari or accessing the online edition,
please e-mail customer-service@safaribooksonline.com